Story Poems From a Western Colorado Boyhood

By Thomas Davis

Story Poems from
a Western Colorado Boyhood

an autobiography in verse

Thomas Davis

Four
Windows
Press

Four Windows Press

Sturgeon Bay, WI 54235

fourwindowspress1@gmail.com

Four Windows Press
Thomas Davis
231 N. Hudson Ave.
Sturgeon Bay, WI 54235

Publisher's Note: This is a work of poetry. Names, characters, places, and incidents are a product of the author's memory and imagination. Locales and public names are sometimes used for atmospheric purposes.

Book Layout © 2017 BookDesignTemplates.com

Story Poems from a Western Colorado Boyhood -- 1st ed.
ISBN - 979-8-9905946-2-3

Note on Cover Photograph: The photograph is of Red Mountain between Ouray and Silverton Colorado. It was taken by Kevin Michael Davis (Alazanto) our beloved son before he passed from cancer in Poughkeepsie, NY at the age of 27.

Dedication

To Mildred Hart Shaw, whose mentorship allowed me to become a poet and writer.

Ethel Mortenson, whose appearance in my life ended my boyhood and has continued to enrich my life to this day.

Acknowledgments

"The Great Comic Book Battle," *Moss Piglet*, John Bloner, ed., September 2022, pp. 78-82.

"Confronting the Buffalo," Unknotting the Line: The Poetry in Prose, David Meischen and Scott Wiggerman, eds. (Albuquerque, New Mexico: Dos Gatos Press, 2023), p. 44.

"David Winger and I sat on a foothill looking out," *Moss Piglet*, January 2020, John Bloner, Jr., ed., p. 62.

"Library in the Canyon" The Zuni Mountain Poets, Jack Carter-North, Margaret Gross, and Thomas Davis eds. (Bloomington, Indiana: iUniverse Press, 2012), p. 144.

"The Storm," *Moss Piglet*, March 2024, John Bloner, Ed., pp. 63-64.

"Genius: Mildred and Bill," 2015 Wisconsin Poets' Calendar, Jean Tomasko and Steve Tomasko, ed. (Eau Claire, Wisconsin: Wisconsin Fellowship of Poets, 2014).

"Cryptic Moon," *The Lyric*, Vol. 97, No.1, Summer 2017, p. 91.

"A Lover's Song," *The Lyric*, Vol. 96, No. 2, Spring 2016, p. 46.

"The Poet and the Artist," *Moss Piglet*, March 2025, John Bloner, Ed.

I owe a lot to both the *Zuni Mountain Poets*, which Ethel and I were a part of every Sunday during the years we lived in Continental Divide, New Mexico and *Unabridged*, poets from Sturgeon Bay, Wisconsin where we now live. Most of these poems were written in New Mexico, but several were composed in Sturgeon Bay. All benefited from the analysis made by these two groups of outstanding poets. I owe a special thanks to Mike Orloch who helped me edit this manuscript, getting rid of my typos and grammar errors.

Cover Photo: "Red Mountain" by Kevin Michael Davis
Cover Design: Ethel Mortenson Davis

CONTENTS

An Old Man's Applause

I was seven years old.
Mom insisted I was too sick to play an old man in a fake gray beard,
but I had worked hard to memorize my school play's lines.
I was so sick I could hardly get out of bed.
I got up anyway, dressed in old man clothes
mom had stitched out of dad's cast-off pants and shirts
and walked out of the house through darkened streets to Delta
      Elementary.

Back stage I half fainted when I saw
the auditorium packed with kids, parents, and grandparents.
Other kids and our teacher just accepted I was there.
Feverish, I feverishly repeated lines over and over in my head
and fought my stomach's queasiness.

Then the play about pioneering, wagon trains, and wilderness began.
When my turn came, I walked, teetering,
the way I was supposed to, on stage.
My mom had no idea where I was.
An old man, I sat on a stool covered with a painted cardboard stump,
voice quavering as if I was sixty years old and not just sick.
When I finished, the audience broke into thundering applause.

I bowed quickly, went off-stage, down ancient wooden stairs,
and went outside where the Milky Way flowed light toward the
      horizon.

What Happened at Delta Elementary School In 1956

Our parents hated Elvis Presley, especially in Delta Colorado.
He swiveled his hips and bellowed rock music
(who'd ever heard of rock music anyway?)
and gyrated around the stage like a crazy man.

Then, one day at Delta Elementary School,
this sixth grader was out on the playground
and started fooling around, swiveling his hips
and gyrating like a crazy man, singing just like Elvis Presley.
He'd slicked back his hair and sounded really wild.

The principal saw this sixth grader I didn't know,
got bug eyes: *What would parents say*
If they heard was happening at Delta Elementary?
and told the kid to stop, but the kid wouldn't and crooned,

> *Let's rock*
> *Everybody, let's rock*
> *Everybody in the whole cell block*
> *Was dancin' to the Jailhouse Rock*

                                        swiveling his hips.

The principal, face getting red, shouted,
then grabbed the kid and hauled him off to the office.

Then the kids around the kid that had been singing
stopped what they were doing and watched the kid
being dragged up concrete stairs into the school.
They were quiet for a moment, and then one girl,
looking mad, started saying softly, *Elvis, Elvis.*

Pretty soon the kids around that kid
were saying *Elvis, Elvis* but louder and louder.
The rest of us didn't know what was going on,
but the whole playground, even the first graders,
started drifting toward that group.

Pretty soon every kid in the school was chanting
Elvis, Elvis at the top of their lungs.
When the teachers monitoring everybody
tried to get the kids chanting to stop,
everybody started dancing and screaming.

When things got so wild teachers were frantic,
the kid came out of the school without the principal
and stood at the top of the concrete steps.

He looked at everybody a minute.
Slowly, the playground grew silent.

The kid held his hand up in the air.
Then, gyrating his hips, sang,

Well, it's one for the money two for the show
Three to get ready now go, cat, go

and all the kids started shouting and dancing around,
and even some of the teachers joined the mayhem.

A Fisherman's Tale

When dad told me we were moving out of Delta,
I was at the grocery store on Main Street,
knowing the Renfrows next door had ended the lease
that let my dad and mom operate the store.
I was candling eggs after my mom had cleaned them
to make sure there wasn't an embryo inside the shell
that would make it unsafe and unsellable.

I was standing on the stool I used to get high enough
to stare through the small hole in the wooden box
to see through the egg's shell and felt disoriented
hearing my dad talking about moving.
I'd lived in Delta all my life along with my two brothers.
We'd leave everything we knew,
although Ronnie was still too young to know anything,
and face the unknown of Orchard Mesa,
a suburb of Grand Junction, a city as unlike Delta
and its comfortable small-town ways as possible.

When my grandma came by the store later that day,
she was carrying a fishing pole
and told Gary and me we were going fishing
by the Gunnison beneath the old Twenty-Five Mesa bridge.
We didn't hesitate but followed her to her car
and piled in, both Gary and I sharing the front seat.
We were as excited as we always were
when grandma decided to take us fishing.

My dad never approved of grandma's ideas about fishing.
He was a trout man who loved going to Grand Mesa
and fishing the streams and lakes teeming with trout.
Grandma, being from Oklahoma,
thought catfish and bass were as good to eat as trout,
making my dad shake his head in disbelief
that anyone, even his wife's mother, could think that.
"Bottom feeders," he'd say. "Nothing but garbage eaters."

I was upset about the idea of moving
as we came to the bridge and parked by the road,

but I didn't say anything.
I wasn't even sure if Gary or grandma had been told.
Dad had just seemed to mention it
as I was staring through a transparent egg good to go.

The three of us climbed down the steep bank
to the Gunnison's edge with our fishing poles
and put worms from grandma's garden on our hooks.
Grandma helped Gary, but I was old enough
to put the worm on without any help.
Then all three of us tossed our lines out
into the swirling drive of the river that ran past Delta
through foothills and canyons toward Grand Junction.

Gary, as usual, caught the first fish, a rainbow trout
my dad would be more than happy to cook up.
Then grandma pulled in a sun fish and then a bluegill.
The upset I was feeling was getting worse
as I thought about what dad had told me
when I finally got a sharp tug on my line,
causing me to jerk the fishing pole back
the way you were supposed to if you wanted to set a hook.

Then a tremendous battle began,
the dream of all fishermen, especially one in the fifth grade.
Seeing what was going on, grandma got excited.

"You got a big one on, Tommy!" she shouted out,
wiping her hands on the flowered dress she was wearing.

The problem was that the fish was bigger
than any fish I'd ever caught.
It seemed heavy, and it kept jerking and jerking,
fighting for freedom I was determined to take away.
I'd tossed the line out further than I ever had before,
and when the fish jumped out of the water
and slipped back into the roiling current it lived in,
it didn't seem to be any closer to the shore
than it had when I'd first hooked it.

As in any good fishing story, as grandma and Gary
urged me on as I tried to bring the fish in,

the fish jumped one more time, the line went slack,
and the biggest fish I ever hooked when I was young
got away.

But it was on a day when I lost more than a fish.
It was on a day when I was frightened
and had no idea what was lying ahead
as the three of us told a story
that sounded like a fisherman's tall tale
but really happened.

The Chili Supper in North Delta

As we got into the station wagon, mom shook her finger at me.
"You got to eat what we're being served for supper," she admonished
    me.
"No whining around because it's not what you're used to."

"Like I always say," my dad chimed in.
"Just remember the starving kids in Africa I saw during the war.
They would've given anything to get anything to eat."

With those words we were off, me in the back seat
wondering why I was being made to go along
to the Mexican community dinner in North Delta
while Gary was left behind at home with a babysitter.
Watching the brand new black and white tv would've been better.

Dad drove across the old silver bridge over the Gunnison River
and parked in front of the dull green North Delta Community Center.
A gadzillion cars were parked outside, most of them old.
My mom firmly took my hand when I started dragging my feet.
I'd been told there would be a lot of Mexican kids,
but, as far as I knew, I didn't know any of them.

Inside Mexican music was swirling
and brown laughing and smiling faces were everywhere.
I didn't see any kids, but I huddled close to my mom
as my dad launched himself into the crowd of men and women,
joining in the talking, joking, and laughing.
He knew a lot of people there, and he was happy.
We'd been the only white people from town invited.

As my mom made her way, with me in tow,
to where one of the Mexican ladies was leading us
to chairs placed behind a large, long table covered
with a colorful checkered oilcloth tablecloth,
I felt small in the crowd of people I didn't know.
I'm sure I had seen many of them
at the grocery store on Main Street as I did my daily chores,
but I had a hard ball in the center of my stomach.

The talking and visiting went on and on,
everybody but me seeming to have a good time,
even my mom who was talking to one lady after another.
My dad, of course, was in his glory with the men.
This was a gathering, and he loved gatherings.

When young ladies started bringing big blue bowls out of the kitchen
and placing them on the checkerboarded tables,
the whole room, including several kids I'd finally spotted,
rustled in what seemed like a single movement to their chairs.
Chili soup in the bowls was steaming,
and the smell of beans, a little beef, and a dark brown soup
had a spiciness that, placed in front of me,
made me squirm in my chair like a chained prisoner.
I hated spicy food!

My mom glared at me, frowning.
"We lost the lease on the Main Street store," she reminded me.
"Our customers are trying to make us feel good," she said.
"Including you.
Don't," she paused. "Embarrass us!"

My dad, who had got his chili before my mom and I did,
dipped his spoon into the soup and took a big bite
with me watching him, resigned to what I had been told to do.
His eyes grew large as he swallowed.
He looked at his neighbor, one of his best Mexican friends,
and exclaimed, "Now that's what I call chili!"
His friend slapped him on the back and laughed
as all the people around us started eating, talking, and laughing.

I looked up at my mom. I didn't say anything,
but I tried to say, Really? with my eyes.
My mom, looking at my dad as he gingerly spooned another bite,
dipped her spoon into the chili and took a sip.
"Don't embarrass us," she whispered to me again.
"These are people that just eat differently from how we eat."

As she sipped on juice from the chili,
her eyes grew as large as my dad's eyes had,
and I got this feeling that maybe I'd never make it to adulthood.

Dread rushing through me, I dipped my spoon into the chili,
stirred the beans, juice, and meat around,
and then slowly brought the spoon to my lips.

Fire! I was expected to eat fire! Fire!

I put the spoon down, looked around at people eating
like they were scoffing down what they ate every day,
and I tried not to look like I was dying and descending into hellfire.
My dad didn't pay any attention to me at all,
but my mother, taking another cautious bite of her chili,
was watching me, and I could tell she was thinking.

"A lot of jalapeno peppers in this," she remarked softly.

Looking in consternation at her, I thought her eyes might be watering.

Swallowing, I took a big spoonful of the fire,
put the spoon in my mouth, closed my eyes, and swallowed.
I sputtered, coughing and half choking, as I prepared to meet my maker
even though I had only just graduated from fifth grade.

My dad didn't notice, although I'm pretty sure some of those
around me saw how I was acting.
Nobody said anything, though. They just went on eating the fiery chili.
My mom, though, put her hand on my hand holding the spoon.

"I guess it's pretty hot," she said. She smiled.
"Maybe you'd better not try to eat anymore."

Then she looked at the community hall's ceiling toward heaven
and carefully brought her spoon to her mouth.

Confronting the Buffalo

I trailed behind the rest of the scouts. I shouldn't have, and one of the leaders should have been watching, but it was blazing hot and summer sun shimmered light above the floor of Ute Canyon. We'd climbed down off the rim and were hiking the canyon's length to the huge chain link fence between the park border and the Redlands. The water in my silver canteen already tasted hot. I wasn't up to such a long, difficult hike. I'd only been out of the body cast for a couple of weeks, but I kept thinking, *I can do this*—determined to be part of the scout troop's adventures. When I noticed I couldn't see any scouts ahead of me, I thought, *You'd better get a move on.* But I was having trouble moving through the heat.

A raven landed on the desiccated gray branch of a dead juniper ahead of me, and I stopped, startled. Silence, not a breeze, not the sound of an insect inside the canyon's sandstone walls, not the sound of talking or laughter. Sighing, I forced myself forward and breathed relief when the raven took off, the sound of wings dissipating the feeling of deadness.

I hadn't taken a dozen steps when I made my way around a clump of sagebrush and was confronted by an old bull buffalo. I could smell his musk. He had a massive head with shaggy, dark brown fur—horns menacing, dark brown eyes glaring at me as heat rose in waves off his body. I stood paralyzed as the huge beast stared at me. I was alone. I was lost. I had a buffalo bull between me and the only people who knew where I was.

The Great Comic Book Battle

A knight, silver armor shining, riding a huge white war horse
through gnarled peach tree branches, jangled in morning sunlight.
Twelve-year-olds, eyes wide as saucers, watched the specter as he rode.

Then the great knight was gone. Yelling boys and girls
were in an empty lot overgrown with weeds taller than they were,
swinging wooden swords and shouting as battle's din
spilled rivers of blood into dry Colorado soil.
Heroes and heroines reigned triumphant
with victories against terrible foes dark as midnight, spewing despair.

Then David Winger, Larry Vertree, my brother, the Manspeakers clan,
    and I
were found by the Maybury brothers, and the great battle stopped.

"You want to see my comic collection?" Bob Maybury asked, towering
    over us.
No one trusted Bob Maybury.

"Why?" David Winger asked. "You've never let us see it before."

But we'd heard about it.
The rumor was that Bob had so many comics in his room
you wove a path through them to his bed.
To kids submerged in the romance of being heroes and heroines,
saving the world over and over again,
filled with stories that bubbled out of the roots of peach orchards,
Bob Maybury's comic trove almost made him and his brothers, Tim
    and Richard,
seem like something other than the bullies they were.

Bob stretched, a sinuous serpent in afternoon sun, and smiled.
"But I'm going to let you see it today," he said.

We looked at each other. Desire and avoidance pulled in opposite
    directions.
"Naw," Larry, my best friend said. "We got stuff to do."
"What stuff?" Tim asked. "Just stuff," Larry said stubbornly.
"What's the catch?" Louella Manspeaker asked.

"You always want something. You don't give anything away."
Louella had just turned thirteen, was taller than the rest of us,
and had a practical bent that made her think
she was better than the little kids she hung around with.

Bob smiled again. "I'm giving you one chance," he said.
"There won't be another one.
If you aren't interested and want to play silly games, that's okay with
     me."
He shrugged and started walking back to Orchard Street and home.
Tim and Richard followed him.

"Wait!" I called out. I felt like what I thought feeling drunk would feel
     like.

Tim stopped and looked at me. Bob and Richard kept walking.
"Yeah?" Tim asked.
"You're making a mistake, Tommy," Louella warned.
"But all those comics," David breathed. "We'll never get another
     chance."

Tim waited. I looked at Larry, David, and my brother Gary.
Gary, smallest and boldest of us, walked toward Tim.
"What are we afraid of?" he asked.
"They do anything we'll take off like a flock of mallards. They'll never
     catch us."

David, Larry, and I hung back,
but I got to thinking about how I couldn't let Gary go off with the
     Maybury's alone.
What would mom and dad say? Especially mom.
Then I was running with David and Larry to catch up.
The Manspeakers followed too, but further back—
to protect our retreat after inevitable disaster.

Outside the Maybury house we stopped when Tim opened the door.
Bob and Richard were inside waiting.

"What's wrong?" Tim sneered. "You guys afraid of the Maybury
     brothers?"
Gary startled. He wasn't afraid of anything.

David, Larry, and I followed him, three lemmings moving toward an
     Alaskan cliff.
Manspeakers gathered on the street just out of the Maybury's yard.
Inside the house Tim led us to Bob's room.
Sure enough, rumors were close to truth.
Comics were scattered in piles that lined the walls.
There were hundreds of them!
The only problem was that Bob, Richard, and Tim weren't smiling.
Tim had fallen behind us just as we got to Bob's room and shut the
     door.

"What do you think of my collection?" Bob asked.

I looked at the comics. Wings grew on my back
and launched me above a prehistoric village
as a Tyrannosaurus towered above immense trees.
"Wow," I breathed.

Bob smiled. "Well," he said expansively. "Here's what we're gonna do.
Old man Wesley's traded that '49 Chevy he doesn't drive anymore for
     these comics.
The thing's a heap, but Richard and I figure we can get it running."
He paused. "In return for letting you see my trove,
you guys are going to help us deliver the comics
to Wesley's house across Highway 51 so I can get my car."
He'd crossed arms across his chest, looking as mean as he knew how to
     look.

Gary, bold as ever, looked up into Bob's threatening eyes and shook
     his head.
"Why should we do that?" he asked. "That's work, and you're getting
     the car."

Richard laughed, his face dark and menacing.
Bob and Gary stared at each other without blinking. Bob smiled.
I felt like grabbing Gary's arm and running,
forgetting about the comic treasure trove forever.
Not only was carrying piles of comics to the Wesley house a lot of
     work,
but crossing 51 loaded with comics that could blow away in the wind
as semi after semi rumbled past wasn't exactly safe.

I could already hear the lecture mom would make dad give Gary and
    me.
"Let's put it this way," Bob growled.
"I've always wanted to break a little Davis's arm
just to hear how a bone sounds when it's breaking."

I grabbed Gary's arm and tugged him close to me.
"What you want us to do?" I asked Bob.
Bob shrugged. "Pick up a pile of comics," he said.
"Old man Wesley thinks this collection might be worth something
    someday,
and I need wheels."

"You need wheels?" Larry asked, half sneering.
"I thought you, Richard, and Tim needed wheels."

Bob shook his head. "Think you can split up three brothers?" he asked.
"I'm the one with the driver's license.
They can come with me, but the wheels will be mine. Now move."

He grabbed my arm and squeezed hard, but I didn't cry out.
He pushed me toward comic books.
I started gathering Superman and the Green Hornet, stacking them
so that I could carry them for a little over a mile.
Gary, David, and Larry followed my example, cowed by Bob's threats.
Pretty soon Richard and Tim were escorting us out into afternoon
    sunshine.

When we walked out the front door, I felt Louella's look, saying, "I told
    you so."

David, Larry, Gary, and I trudged down Orchard Street,
chained slaves walking toward certain doom.

We were passing the empty weed lot where we fought our most
    glorious battles
when the shining knight appeared.
Louella had put a silver bowl over her head and had a stick sword in
    her hand.
Her two brothers and two sisters were standing behind her.

"For freedom, human dignity, and justice!" she shouted.

I stopped. David, Gary, and Larry stopped.

"Oh no!" Richard chortled. "You little kids slay me!"
I looked at Louella, feeling a strength I never knew I had flowing into
    me
and tossed comics as wind blew them down Orchard Street.

"Mallards fly!" Gary shrieked.
David and Larry shouted battle cries as more comics were thrown into
    the wind.

"Bastards!" Richard shouted.
His and Tim's face looked dark as midnight, evil with rage.
Both lunged toward me, Gary, David, and Larry.
Louella, wielding her stick sword, charged.
"For freedom!" I screamed.

Then all of us were running, throwing taunts at dragons
belching flames as they scorched burning earth.

Minutes after chortling our great victory over terrible forces of
    darkness,
we headed home, knowing we'd have to stay there
until the Maybury's calmed down, and it became safe enough to again
hide in a peach orchard while watching a shining knight
and his great white war horse jangle through the trees.

How Elk Came to the Colorado Mountains

Andy McLean told the story. He was already old,
his good-humored energy making him comic
as he walked bow-legged and bright eyed, face ravaged by time.

We had been at elk camp above Meeker for a week.
My mom, aunts, older women, and girl cousins got up before dawn
to fix black coffee, bacon, hash browns, and eggs over campfires.
Men checked 30-30s and 30-06s and prepared for hillsides
where aspens fluttered intensely yellow above paper-white trunks.
Breakfast done, men, women, boys, and girls climbed into pickup
    trucks,
or rode one of Uncle JT's sorrel horses,
down boulders masquerading as roads into wilderness.

That morning, dusk smoky with first light, a shot rang out
as we prepared to slough off the road to go to hunting spots
where we hoped we'd find an old bull with branching horns
and dark chest fur walking calmly into a fall grasses meadow.
Later we found out two old men had got in a fight the night before
sitting by a campfire drinking blackberry brandy.
In pre-dawn the younger brother had got up angry
and walked to a clearing a quarter a mile from their camp
and shot his older brother's white mule.

None of our family knew what had happened until we'd hunted
    hard all day,
climbing up and down hills and sitting on stones and rotted pine
    tree trunks
in thin mountain sun, looking and looking for elk that never came.
When Uncle JT called a halt as sunset blazed red. orange, and
    reddish purple,
I walked behind a small stand of scrub oak on my way to the truck.
A five-point buck fed not twenty feet away out of season and safe.

When we got back to camp, finished eating food sizzled off
    campfires,
and sat, backs against trees, on the ground,

leaving camp chairs for mothers, grandparents, and fathers,
Andy McLean, the oldest person there, told his story.
"Elk weren't always common in the mountains," he said as he
    started.
"They were a plains animal that grazed the great prairies."

His voice was soft, though it had a story-teller's lilt,
and some of the grandparents had to strain to hear.
The moment he'd started camp noise,
clattering forks against tin dishes, walking around, laughter, talking,
    stopped,
and I, my brothers, mom, dad, aunts, uncles, grandparents, and
    cousins
listened.

"I was working for Colorado Fish and Game back then," Andy
    continued,
"And my boss, Roy Smith, a good old boy who was always spitting
    tobacco,
told me to take a train to Kansas and bring elk back to transplant in
    the mountains.

"I was young, fuller of myself than I had any right to be,
convinced I was God's gift to ladies, government, and every man I
    met.
Roy had hardly told me I was going on a trip
before I'd saddled Barney, my spirit paint, planted both of us in a
    cattle car,
and was off to Kansas to find out what an elk was.

"The first time I saw a bunch of elk I wasn't impressed.
They were big, and the bulls had impressive horns,
but twenty-three had been corralled in a Salina cattle feedlot.
They were tied to posts to keep them from jumping fences
built way too low to hold an animal like that,
and they looked bedraggled and dispirited. Pitiful."

Andy chuckled to himself and tipped back his cowboy hat,
a brown Stetson battered and stained from years of use.

"I was a damned fool when I was young," he said to himself.
Then he laughed, making everyone in camp smile.

"Anyway," he continued. "A bunch of boys and I looked at those
    elk
and figured we could get on our horses
and herd them to cattle cars the way we herded cows or horses.
A foreman came out of the cattle feedlot's office and set us straight:
'You do that, boys,' he said, 'you'll be fired, and the world wants
    your job.
Truth is no man alive is going to herd a herd of elk.
Two men have got to get a rope around each of them
and drag them to where they least want to go,
and let me tell you, boys. Two horses and two men ain't enough.'

"A bunch of young cowboys, tough as nails
and more experienced than any other group of cowboys could be,
    scoffed.
I listened to what the foreman said, whipped out my rope,
and lassoed the biggest bull before anyone else moved.
Another man went over to untie the brute from its post
as the animal's eyes whited panic and started pulling.
A second later Barney and I were in trouble as that old bull thrashed
    and pulled.
Rope burned my hands through leather gloves,
and the bull started to leap away into town, and then prairie
where it thought it belonged, taking my job with its flight to
    freedom.
It was the depression, and I needed that job.

"Luckily, three more ropes snaked air behind mine,
one got the bull's hind leg, and pretty soon a couple of us
were wrangling the animal toward its destined rail car.
By the time we had twenty-three elk in three cars with the doors
    shut,
eight cowboys were tired and sheepish.
A handful of wild animals had worn us out and tamed us.

"The trip to Colorado was okay.
The elk were scared, and keeping them watered and fed was a chore,
but Jim Hornsby, the man hired to help me, and I were used to that
    work.
It was when we got to Ouray, I discovered how much a fool I really
    am.

Jim and I got to talking about how hard those elk were to corral in
    Kansas
as the narrow gauge steamed up-valley from Montrose to Ouray,
and we decided that since our job was to get elk into mountains,
all we had to do when we got to Ouray was to open cattle car doors
and let them bound into their new home.

What we didn't count on was the band that met us at the train
    station
decked out in their Sunday's finest to see these new creatures
that were going to make the San Juan Mountains home.
I especially didn't count on Zelda May Pinchot, the Mayor's wife,
and her garden filled with a rainbow of gladiolas.

"The train pulled into the station, the band started playing,
Jim and I ignored everybody as we opened car doors,
and not a single elk moved toward town streets and freedom.
Steam-hissing train, billows of smoke, blaring band,
and brightly colored clothes of the women
spooked and drove them back against the cattle car's far wall.

I'm afraid I said a word or two that shouldn't be heard by children."
He looked around at me and my cousins, smiled, then went on.

"Miss Zelda heard what I said, her face got red, and she started
    toward me,
leaving the mayor and other town folks behind.
She was a formidable woman, not five foot tall, but stout,
with eyes that blazed like a red sun at sunrise.
I didn't see her coming. I'd climbed up into the car,
holding the big bull that had made a fool of me in Salina,
determined to make something happen and end the farce.
As I walked up to that huge animal and the cows around him,
he stopped shuffling, lowered horns bigger than the rail car's
    insides,
and charged me as I jumped back and away, heart hammering.
The bull leapt out of the cattle car, followed by its cows.
Miss Zelda shrieked, fell in the dirt with her new dress.
Everybody else got busy dodging leaping elk,
and twenty-three animals headed toward becoming the mountain
    animals they are.

"I got up, dazed from my brush with horned death,
just as the big bull jumped over a white picket fence and led a herd
through the mayor's wife's prized gladiola garden."

Andy stopped and shook his head.
He was silent for so long, my cousins and I started to fidget.
The story didn't seem to be quite over, but it sounded like it was
    over.
At last, my dad, black eyes shining in firelight, asked,
"But what happened then, Andy?"

Andy looked abstractly at the camp, including the whole family in a
    single look.
We were together then, generations of Davises, Jackses, and
    Morrises,
all of us bound by a story and an elk camp above Meeker
beside a big campfire burning beneath stars and a yellow half-moon.

"I didn't lose my job," Andy said. "And that was good because in
    those days,
as some of you know, a job kept you from riding the rails looking
    for work.
But when the mayor had helped his wife get up out of the dust,
and Miss Zelda saw what those elk had done to her gladiolas,
well…." He stopped speaking again.

"Well, what?" my cousin Stella Louise, Uncle JT's oldest, demanded.

Andy looked at Stella Louise, smiled gently, firelight flickering on
    his face,
and said, "Well, young lady, at your age, you don't want to know."

Aunt Viola went to her daughter and put her hand on her shoulder,
and the elk camp started stirring toward sleeping bags and bed.

The Kingdom of Grand Mesa

My brother Gary got Andy MacLean to tell the story.
We had given up bank-fishing Ward, Twin, and Alexander Lakes
and moved to the stream that fed Alexander.
We hadn't done that bad. I'd caught a brookie and two rainbow trout.
My brother Ronnie, even younger than we were,
had done better, filling his creel with six rainbows,
but Gary had not had a good day at all.
He'd caught two suckers and had to throw back two rainbow
    fingerlings.
When he caught a third sucker he threw his hat on the ground, and
    said,
"Damned! We should have gone to the Cottonwoods.
These are the worst fishing holes on Grand Mesa!"

We hadn't seen Andy MacLean coming with his battered felt cowboy
    hat
and bowlegged gait, curious to see what trouble we had made for
    ourselves,
but he was close enough to hear Gary,
and he laughed as he climbed to where we were standing.

"Boring place, eh boys?" he asked good naturedly.
"A good place for suckers!" Gary grumbled, pointing at the gasping
    fish
he'd thrown on the bank to reduce the population polluting
    Alexander's waters.

Andy touched Gary's shoulder. "I suppose mom's looking for us,"
    Ronnie said,
contemplating the wisdom of taking off upstream
and letting Andy say he couldn't find the youngest Davis.

Andy smiled, "No, no," he said. "I was just wondering how you guys
    were doing.
I've been skunked all day and was tired of staring at a slack line in the
    water."

"Like I said," Gary complained. "We should have gone to the
    Cottonwoods!"

Andy pursed his lips and looked at Gary.
Sun was shining, stream waters singing, and life was good.
Andy sat down on the hillside above Gary and me.
"Oh, this is a good area," he said. "Sometimes a place is more than
      fishing."
Gary and Ronnie looked doubtful, but I could see the story
taking shape in Andy's head as clearly as if I could read his thoughts.
I climbed up beside him and found a large volcanic rock to sit on.

"Don't suppose you guys ever heard the story of Alexander Lodge,"
      Andy said.
"Or of how most of Grand Mesa's lakes got here.
Folks around here don't want to hear the story,
especially if their family's been around Delta and Grand Mesa for a
      long time.
But that story hangs around Ward, Twin, and Alexander
like smoke hangs around a fire."

Ronnie, always ready to hear a story, put down his fishing pole
and came to sit beside me. Gary, disgusted with fishing, sat below us.

"What happened," Andy continued, "was that a man by the name of
      Alexander
came to Delta driving a fancy buckboard wagon over roads not fit for a
      horse.
By then womenfolk had begun to move into Grand Valley,
but it was still wild. Men wore guns in holsters threaded into belts,
and folks thought a man could do as he pleased unless he got shot or
      laid up.
Most people living here were ranchers,
though Delta already had a boarding house, a saloon, and a couple of
      stores—
a few were starting to farm.

"Anyway," Andy said. "Alexander came dressed in fancy eastern dud
      clothes
with a brogue so thick you could almost tell he was speaking English.
He claimed he was Scottish royalty fleeing,
from a love affair with a dark, exotic woman,
to the wild west to forget his sorrows.
Nobody believed him. Folks were poor, and nobody could figure out
why anybody would leave a Scottish castle behind,

love affair or no love affair.
"The early settlers took Grand Mesa for granted.
The mountain was a fisherman's and hunter's paradise,
and if they needed a change in diet, a day away from the world's cares,
or just wanted to contemplate how beautiful the earth could be,
they'd ride up green slopes to fish lakes or streams or get meat for the
        table."
Andy paused to gather his thoughts.

"Was this Duke Alexander a bad man?" Ronnie asked.
Andy laughed. "A bad man?" he said, considering the question.
"I think he was American through and through.
He came from Scotland, though later people doubted that.
He was a mystery, but he was American in spirit if not in fact."

He paused, looking at our faces' puzzlement, and went on:
"The minute Alexander set eyes on Grand Mesa he wanted to own it.
Aspen trees, pine forests, streams, lakes, trout, and wild game made it
        paradise,
and Alexander was a determined man.

"His first idea was to put together an army that could seal off the
        mountain,
ending the fishing, hunting, and picnicking
ranchers and townspeople thought were their right for pioneering.
The problem was that he could only get a couple of the wilder men
to work for him once people got to know what he was after,
and he didn't feel any safer around them than anybody else.
Then he got the idea that he should build a magnificent lodge
and dam the streams right where we are sitting.
He was going to build lakes, talk the railroad into extending a spur into
        Delta,
and then refrigerate railroad cars so he could take trout
out of the lakes he'd made and ship them to Chicago and Kansas City
as a luxury food that would increase his fortune ten-fold.

"When he spread that dream around a few started coming over to his
        side.
His money was good,
and he was willing to pay wages nobody in Delta had earned before.
A railroad spur might make the town boom and improve townspeople's
        lives.

So, the Duke began building the first Alexander Lodge,
and he started on a grand tour to the Midwest and East
to raise capital, talk the railroad into coming to Delta,
and find markets for fish fresh from the Colorado Rockies.

"He was gone for months, but when he returned, he was triumphant.
He said he'd gotten everything he could have dreamed of from his trip,
and he was going to turn Grand Mesa into a kingdom.
He bragged that his dark woman was going to join him
now that he was more important than she had thought he would be.
Four months after coming back he had forty men on his payroll,
and the carpenters and workers he'd hired had not only built his lodge,
but had also built dams to create Alexander, Ward, and Twin Lakes.
It was at that point things started to get interesting."

"I'll bet," Gary said dryly. "Ssshhh," Ronnie and I, captivated, said at
       once.
Andy was no longer smiling, but looked as if the sunny day
was about to turn dangerous with black clouds, thunder, and lightning.

"The problem," he continued. "was that not long after the lakes were
       built,
Alexander went back to his first plan.
He sent horsemen out to patrol Grand Mesa's slopes
while he sat in his castle of a lodge plotting his future.
He told his men to keep cowboys and townspeople off land
he claimed he'd secured from the government."

Andy looked at us, eyebrows wrinkled together on his forehead.
"What you boys don't know is how riled up folks can get
when they feel a Scottish Duke has taken what's theirs with a hired
       army.
Ranchers and townspeople started meeting,
talking about how what Alexander was doing wasn't right.
No one had trusted the man from the minute he had set foot in town.
He'd used smooth words to hoodwink them into believing
his fortune was their fortune, and now they were angry
down into the core of who they were as Westerners.

"Talk went on for a month. Then, on a Sunday,
a mob of over a hundred men gathered near Cedaredge.

They had rifles and pistols, and when they'd worked themselves up
     enough,
they rode toward Alexander's new lodge
determined to drive the Scotsman back to Scotland.
Alexander's men saw them coming and hightailed to their boss.
He told them to defend his territory like it was their kingdom.
The carpenters and workmen, hearing what was up,
knowing they had relatives marching up the mountain, took to the
     woods.
Those left decided to make a stand upslope from the Delta mob
to see if guns and the advantage of height would scare them off.

"Not an hour later the battle was over.
One of Alexander's men, building his courage with whiskey,
saw the Delta men riding toward the group he was with
and started whooping and hollering and spurring his horse
toward men tense with the idea that they might die
to do right by Grand Valley's people and their traditions.
Ten rifles barked and shot him from his saddle,
killing his horse and leaving him wounded and bleeding.
Alexander's army took off and was never seen again.

"Alexander, dreams disappearing like smoke from ten rifles,
took off too, leaving his grand lodge and lakes behind.
The mob kept moving up the mountain to the lodge.
They lit torches and started drinking.
They burned the picture Alexander had had painted of his dark lady
and then fired the lodge and workmen's and army's cabins.
The party went on all night and half the next day
until men were sprawled senseless along Alexander Lake's shores."

Andy finished, staring down at his hands.
He looked as if the pain in his story had gotten into him.

"Wow," Gary said. "That must have been some party."

"A man died," Andy said, not looking up from his hands.
"That man would have been my uncle if I had been born."

"Oh," Gary said.

The story had taken so long the sun was setting.

Pitch black mountain night was in evening shadows.
The land had changed, I thought to myself.
I'd always thought of Alexander Lake as the boring part of Grand
      Mesa.
I would have liked to have gone with Gary to the Cottonwoods.

"It's getting dark," I said. "We've got a hike back to camp.
I don't suppose any of us have a flashlight."
Andy got up and smiled. "You're a smart boy, Tommy," he said.

We crossed the stream we'd been fishing
and walked through a forest that had once been a kingdom—
liberated by the ranchers and townspeople of Delta, Colorado.

Sweat Pours Down Your Back

Clouds, etched white against sky deepening blue,
billowing crests shining defined edges with intense light,
covered half the sky and left sky above my head
blazing, humidity so high carved pieces of wood
we called boats when we were kids
as we put them into dirty canal water running downhill
could have floated on empty air.

Peach orchards, growing out of time, grow brown bodies
that put fat peaches still three quarters ripe in buckets
hung around necks as if heavy necklaces.
I try to keep up with hands filling bucket after bucket.
Peach fuzz gets under my shirt, sweat itching
worse than mosquito bites all over my chest and back.

My mother, eyes squinting, puts the gray vacuum hose
into my body cast and turns the vacuum on full blast.
I frown so hard my mom says,
"You keep doing that your face is gonna freeze.
Then what you going to do when you want to smile?"

I get a hit at an Old Timer's game in Delta where I was born.
I never get a hit! I run to first base.
The guy that wants us to lose so our team captain,
his former best friend, suffers crushing defeat,
screams at me to keep going when I am safe on first base.
Wanting approval, I keep running, a human turtle.
The outfielder picks up the ball and throws it to second.
The ball skitters, "Run!" the traitor I'm trying to get to like me,
even though he'll never like me, screams, and I run
as the pitcher throws to third where the ball sails into the outfield.
"Run!" screams the traitor angry at his best friend,
and I go for home! I never get on first base!
The catcher smiles as the ball claps his glove
and laughs at how I'm trying to score a home run.

Time passes. Old age creeps into who we are.

North sky clouds billow white light. Sun blazes above my head.

What does it mean, running for homebase?
Childhood images tumbling as clouds shine?
Sweat pouring down your back and chest out of your lifetime?

Unintended Consequence

1

A ninth grader in crowded halls at Franklin Junior High said "Hi,"
and I responded, barely looking at him, "Hi."
He went past in the stream of students,
and I didn't think about him again until the next morning.
I was the last one off the bus and was lagging,
especially after the pile of books I was carrying beneath my right arm
    slipped.
I stopped and readjusted them so they wouldn't spill on the ground.
Before I could get to the sidewalk leading to double doors into the
    school,
the ninth grader appeared: a giant.

"Come on, shrimp," he said in a rough voice.
He dragged me off the sidewalk to a corner
creating an alcove where you had to look around red brick
to see where we were, my back to the wall,
his body between me and the lawn in front of the school.

"Think you're pretty smart, don't you?" he sneered. "Shrimp!"
He pushed me, hard, banging my back against the wall.
I was so scared I had no idea what to say or do.
"Shrimp!" he exclaimed again. He shoved me hard again.
The only time I'd ever noticed him was when he'd said "Hi"
as we went opposite ways in streams of students toward our classes.

"What did I do to you?" I asked.
"Shut up, shrimp!" he said,
then shoved me hard against the wall again,
slamming my head against the rough red brick.
My head rang. Black stars swam in front of my face.
I started to cry.

"Shrimp!" he exclaimed again.
He put his face an inch from my face and glared.
"You avoid your betters," he said. "We don't like shrimps."

He turned away from me and was gone,
leaving me crying alone in the corner.

2

A week later I was in downtown Grand Junction walking down Main
      Street.
I wasn't doing anything, just walking in the sunshine.
Suddenly, without warning, seven boys surrounded me,
five Italians I hadn't seen at school and two young blacks.

"Hi," one of the black kids said, walking next to where I was walking.
I didn't answer. I'd learned what saying "Hi" could get you at school.

I felt the black kid's eyes on my face. He looked puzzled.
"Can't talk?" he asked.
I didn't say anything but started walking faster,
wanting to get away from the gang surrounding me.
"What's wrong with you?" one of the Italians asked in an aggressive
      voice.

I still didn't say anything.
We came to the corner of Fifth and Main that had a stop light.
The light was red, so, heart in my throat, I stopped.

"Why won't you talk to me?" the black kid who'd said "Hi" said.
He sounded angry.
I stared at the bank building across the street.
Then the black kid was in front of me with a balled-up fist.
He hit me in the stomach so hard I bent over double
and fell to the sidewalk.

"Racist!" the black kid shouted.
Then the whole group of them were running across the street
toward the corner drug store and alley where they could disappear.

I kept clutching my stomach but finally got to my feet.
I hadn't told my mom or dad about the ninth grader.
I wouldn't tell anybody about this either, I thought to myself.

Skinners

We would get off the school bus,
climb slowly down the hill to my dad's grocery store, Davis Supermarket,
say hi to my mom at the checkout counter
and my dad in the butcher's shop,
then climb down dingy, dusty back stairs to the basement.
There were always two to ten deer or an elk or two
hoisted to the ceiling by my dad using small pulleys before we got home.
He let us sell the hides if hunters from California, Texas, Colorado, or
    places elsewhere failed to ask for them,
and for two teenagers, money was always welcome.
After cleaning the animals and skinning them,
filling the basement with the smell of burnt hair and raw meat
after we had whisked a small propane torch over the carcasses to singe
    away deer or elk hair,
we'd head for the house where mom had cooked supper.
Working from seven to ten-thirty at the store
and then, during the four-month hunting season,
until 2:00 a.m. in the processing plant with its shiny silver saws and
    golden butcher blocks,
my dad always left the store to his lone employee, Jewel,
a small woman who lived next to our house
and had hundreds of marigolds planted in her meticulously "kept-up"
    yard,
for "supper with the family."

During deer or elk season we didn't get much sleep,
even though my dad kept saying Gary and I
would sleep through an earthquake bringing a roof down on our heads.
After supper we'd go back to the basement,
put on green grocer's aprons and start helping dad and mom slice
    carcasses
into steaks, chops, ribs, roasts, and hamburger.
I boned, put suet into the resulting scraps of meat, and ground
    hamburger,
helping mom wrap meat in waxy white butcher paper when I was done.
    Gary, less concerned with books, homework, and writing, tended to
        help my dad
cut up the meat with saws and razor-sharp butcher knives.

I think he meant to spend his life in a grocery store
doing what my dad did for a living.

Dad always sent us home a little after midnight,
but he'd be in our rooms the next morning,
getting us out of bed, feeding us breakfast, and leading us to the store
so we could sweep floors and prepare cash registers for the 7:30 opening,
the exact time when the bus pulled up on the hill above the store to begin
    the drive to school.

Gary and I were expert skinners.
For elk we'd get up on step ladders and separate hides from the carcass,
carefully avoiding making a hole in the hide so it wouldn't lose value,
as we worked our way down to the rump with sharp knives and strong
    wrists.
For deer shot and then hung in colder weather,
we would follow the same process, working quickly, meticulously
    downward,
but for warmer carcasses we could bunch the hide in fists
and pull downward, taking off hide as quickly as we could peel a banana.

One day we got home from school and went downstairs and gaped into
    the basement's dimness.
Our Uncle David had gotten a bear permit from Colorado Department
    Fish and Game,
and he'd shot a massive grizzly bear, its odor so strong it gagged us.
On the floor the bear looked too big to hang for skinning,
and we had no idea how to go about skinning a bear,
but Gary, eyes big and filled with hunting dreams
and the outdoor glory where he'd eventually spend most of his life,
decided the two of us were strong enough to do the hanging.
When we tried to drag the carcass to the pulleys, though,
we could hardly budge the massive body.
We grunted and strained, moved it a foot,
and then decided my dad and Uncle David,
a big man who wrestled bulldozers for Mesa County,
would have to hang the carcass for us.
We also decided Uncle David wouldn't trust us with a hide
he'd probably make into a rug.

At supper that night all we could talk about was the bear
and Uncle David's luck

and how neat it was going to be to learn how to skin a bear.
When we finished fried chicken and potatoes with gravy we rushed to
    the basement.
Uncle David was already there, had sawed off the bear's head,
and had, by himself, pulled it up, using the pulleys, as high as he could
    get it.
Its body was angled against the concrete floor.
He was carefully using his big bone-handled hunting knife to skin down
    the massive carcass.
My dad looked at disappointment in Gary's, my, and Ronnie, my
    youngest brother's faces, and smiled.

"Big bear, David," he said.

David glanced at my dad, then Gary, Ronnie, and I.

"The meat'll be strong," he said, "and sweet.
Shouldn't have taken one so big,
but it was the biggest bear I think I've ever seen."

"Gonna mount the head?" my dad asked.

"Give it away," David answered. "It's too big for my small place.
I have a neighbor who wants it.
The guy who owns the peach orchard next door."

"Sounds best," my dad said and motioned to us three boys.
"Don't bother your uncle," he ordered.
"Go play outside. We'll be at the saws soon enough."

We hung our heads.
Uncle David was working carefully through a spot where cold bear lard
    was sticking stubbornly to hide.
He was concentrating so hard he'd forgotten about us.

My dad went upstairs to finish his store day with my mom who had
    already started sweeping the aisles.
We hung around for a moment,
looking at the intensity in our uncle's eyes.
We could imagine him out on the Uncompahgre Plateau, hearing a
    grizzly snorting,
as he tried to see the massive beast prowling through the mountains.

We could imagine ourselves beside him
as the grizzly came out into the open a hundred yards from him,
looking alive, wild, free, and more dangerous than any other creature in
    the mountains.
We heard the shot,
saw the bear stop its movement toward us,
and saw it topple as if it was a mountain collapsing into a landslide.

Then, like we always did,
we obeyed our father and went outside

and began hunting in wild mountains,
looking for bear even bigger than the grizzly
that later that night we'd turn into steaks and roasts
as if it was no different than an elk or a mule deer.

The power wagon chugged like a snuffling bear

Wheels churned down through snow layers
until they reached hard ground,
and then the dark green cab and truck bed jumped
forward, stopping and lurching as it slowly made
its way across cactus flats toward a hill nestled below
a higher hill where aspen provided a place
where we could pitch tents and build a campfire.

There were two of us, Howard Johnson,
a tall, raw boned kid whose uncle, Jeff Burns,
was the government trapper,
a man who caught mountain lions for delivery to zoos,
and I, more bookworm than mountain man.
Howard had decided to go hunting in Snyder Flats,
and I'd eagerly gone along, excited to feel the bite
of winds that could carve drifts six feet high
when snow mostly covered sagebrush on flats empty of trees.

When the power wagon finally climbed the hill
the aspen grove was dark with evening shadows.
By the time we had tents pitched and a fire going
the moon was waxing full, a silver silence
echoed from the universe's blanket of stars.
By the time we crawled into down sleeping bags
neither of us had said a word to each other for hours.

We woke before dawn when first light smudges
dirtied hill horizons east of where we were.
Howard was in a good mood, starting the fire with twigs,
joking about how crazy we had to be
fixing frozen slabs of bacon and bread over a campfire
when we could have been crawling out of bed
in a house filled with civilization's conveniences.

A half hour later, bellies full, fighting cold's numbness,
we were climbing the hill behind our campsite,
fighting through snow that sometimes came up to our waists.

Howard was stronger and broke trail,
but my breath was sharp as I struggled through a morning
so cold air felt like shards of shattered crystal.
Below us drifts danced with swells in a landscape frozen into waves.
We stopped and felt wilderness's immenseness.

"Think we'll see any deer?" I asked. Howard snorted.

"This is Snyder Flats," he said. "We might even see a grizzly."

I nodded, then we set out again, keeping close to the canyon rim,
fighting the sun's glare off glittering snow.
Hours passed. Even Howard was getting tired and irritable.
Not even a jack rabbit exploded from cover.
Noon came and went, the sun blazed orange, yellow, and red
over the western horizon. Cold became more and more intense.
By the time we found our camp again stars were out
and our feet and hands were numb from a breeze
sweeping across flats up into the hills.

The next day was like the first day. We walked and walked,
but if life was in the universe, it was hiding.
We had told our parents we would be gone four days,
and we'd have to spend most of the fourth day
lurching our way down the hill, through the flats to the dirt road
that would lead us back to Grand Junction and home.
Neither my dad nor Jess Burns had approved of going to Snyder Flats,
so, if we were late, they would come looking for us,
and when they found us, we'd both have to face wrath
that would resolve itself into chores best avoided.

As daylight began to wane, we knew we were too far from camp.
We'd plowed through snow with a ferocity that burned lungs
and made even Howard complain about how tired he was.
By the time we gave up hunting and faced the fact
that our grand trip to Snyder Flats was an unredeemable bust,
we were miles from camp, half lost, and on the other side of the canyon
behind the hill that sheltered the hill with our supplies.
As the full moon came up, discouraged, half scared,
we were trying not to fall as we felt our way down the cliff's face.

I had just managed to use cracks to climb down ten feet of sheer rock to stand on solid ground when Howard grabbed my arm.

"Tommy," he whispered.

His voice had an urgency that made my heart thump in my ears.
I looked toward where he was pointing.
Not forty feet away an immense grizzly was shambling
toward where we were standing.
Howard seemed frozen. We both had guns,
but the bear seemed to be the size of two bears.
The moon was so bright you could make out its hump
as it moved toward us, head low to the ground.

What in the hell have I got myself into now? I asked myself silently.
My stomach churned. Queasy. Unstable.
Howard stared at the bear mesmerized.
God let this be all right, I said to myself. Let this be all right.

Howard slowly began to bring his 30.06 to his shoulder.
The bear saw his movement, turned its massive head toward us
and stood on its hind legs
as if making sure it was seeing what it was seeing.

"Holy Jesus," Howard said out loud.

No sound. Only moonlight making night almost as bright as day.

Howard seemed to have forgotten about his gun.
The bear didn't move but kept staring at us.
It was too dark to see its eyes, but we could feel its eyes anyway,
black, red around the edges, intense with anger at humans
and all humans had done to him and his kind.

A movement caught the edges of my eye,
and I glanced from the grizzly to the south.

"Howard," I said.

Howard tried to look at the bear and where I was pointing at the same
        time.
A huge buck was standing in a clearing ten feet from us.
Its massive rack seemed to have a hundred points

sprouting in all directions from where horns grew from his head.
I looked back at the towering grizzly.
It was looking away from us toward the buck.
The buck snorted. The grizzly snorted.
Howard and I stood like ice statues in the bitter cold.

"A cactus buck," Howard said, wonder inside his voice.

The bear whoofed as it fell to four legs.
With a speed that seemed impossible it blurred toward the buck.
The buck leaped backward, seeming to turn in mid-air.
It bounded down the canyon, outpacing the grizzly.
Within seconds the canyon felt empty again.

Neither Howard nor I spoke as we stood in moonlight
looking toward where the grizzly had gone after the buck.

"Damned cold out here," Howard said at last.
"Yeah," I breathed. My legs felt wobbly.
"We'd better get moving," Howard said.

On the cliff rim, looking down into the canyon, still a mile from camp,
cold getting colder and colder, Howard shook his head.

"They'll never believe this happened if we tell them," he said.
"No," I answered. "I don't think I believe it happened."
My stomach was still churning queasily.

We turned and plowed toward the power wagon,
tents flimsy against wilderness, and home.

Snowmass

We hauled out of Grand Junction in the ancient 1951 white Chevy.
Grandpa George had died the year before,
so, there were three boys, mom and dad, and grandma,
the boys so excited they had gotten up before dawn.
The oldest, I was unsure about the trip.
I could have hung out with the guys at home,
but dad was going to take six days from Davis Supermarket on Orchard
    Mesa
and spend time with the family, something he loved,
especially when fishing or hunting was involved, but seldom got to do.

The drive to Snowmass, through canyons and increasingly higher
    mountains,
was spectacular, though that failed to keep Gary and I from pushing
    against each other,
forcing grandma to suggest Ronnie move to the back,
although he was the least trouble to dad's driving because he was so
    small.
Gary got the front seat because I yelped in protest.
I was supposed to be the most grown up as a worldly teenager of thirteen,
but I liked horsing around even though I would have never admitted it.

When we finally got to the ranch where Uncle Harry and Aunt Grace
    lived,
we piled from the car and looked around as if we had lost old eyes and
    put on new ones.
Light was everywhere: Sun glinted off the small stream wandering in
    meadows deep with grass
and reflected from snow slopes above the ranch.
The old ranch house and bunk house where we were going to stay
had halos shimmering above spruce roof shingles.

Aunt Grace had fixed fried chicken, gravy, and gravy-covered green
    beans,
along with an apple pie cooling on the kitchen's windowsill.
Even though we'd eaten sandwiches in the car,
we sat at the kitchen's old table and ate so much we felt slower when we
    moved.

My cousin Wilma was off somewhere,
which was okay with my brothers and I since she was older
and would have tried to keep us out of trouble,
so we had the ranch to ourselves with hundreds of acres, spruce, pine,
    and aspen forests, trout streams, deer and elk, jack rabbits, and birds.
Maybe we'll see a grizzly, we told ourselves excitedly.

Our family had spent plenty of time in mountains,
especially on Grand Mesa where we went fishing whenever dad got the
    chance.
We'd camped out and stayed in Odd Fellows' cabins above Alexander
    Lake
and fished on lakes so remote they seemed like they'd gotten up
and marched from civilization to grow the biggest trout possible.
But the first evening and night on Snowmass was revelation.
Even on Grand Mesa you heard car, truck, or outboard boat motor
    sounds.
Civilization, even at the Granbys, lakes you hiked miles into, enfolded
    consciousness.

At the ranch my uncle was working for absentee owners.
Silence, as stars shined into evening sky, was absolute:
No distant car sounds, no sounds from the next campground or cabin,
no radio music drifting on air—
only silence and the Milky Way smeared with light.
Not even animals rustling silence.

As the sun went down, mountain cold enveloped us.
Silence, stars, and cold drove us inside the bunk house
where we built a fire in a black pot-bellied stove,
our spirits caught by a memory of time before our family was,
wilderness reminding us we were merely humans.

The rest of the week my brothers and I
started mornings at the narrow, deep creek meandering through an aspen
    grove.
We got on our bellies, dangled hands in freezing-cold water,
and tried to work a trick Aunt Grace had told us about.
She said if you held your hand still in the creek, trout would forget your
    hand was there.
If you were quick, you could catch trout with your bare hand.
The problem was that after holding your hand in water long enough

for speckled brook trout to swim near,
fingers numbed and stiffened and refused to do what you wanted them
    to do.
Sometimes you touched a trout, but freezing-cold water was their
    element, not yours.
As you struggled to catch them, they darted and flew above the creek's
    dark-earth bottom.

During the five days we climbed rock faces,
saw elk, with our dad, in pre-dawn after we had hiked miles to see them,
and wandered, enchanted and wrapped in dream.
When time switched from long wonder into time-to-leave,
I knew I had wandered eternity.
Deep grasses and high mountains had seared who I was.

My uncle and aunt stood on the wooden front porch and waved
as we drove from ranch yard to the long dirt road
that led to the highway down mountains, through canyons to home.
Gary and I knelt on the back seat and stared out the car's back window
    at the ranch
receding from regret we felt at leaving it behind.

Crutches

Nights in hospital rooms were over:
Antiseptic smells, constant pain, medicine that took you from yourself,
    fluorescent lights, a bed that cranked up and down.
Now Gary, my brother, and I were sitting on the car porch,
his foot in a cast, agonizing nights of pain behind him,
my leg in a cast so uncomfortable I could hardly move.

"Hunting season starts today," Gary noted with understated
    nonchalance.
 "Yeah," I said, "and we're stuck here in casts."

Gary pointed at the jeep sitting in the driveway.
It hadn't been driven for two months.

"In the hospital Jim Fennell told me hunting's good around Paonia," he
    said.
"He came to see me after he left you."
"And how do we get to Paonia?" I asked. "I can't clutch and step on the
    gas.
We only have two good legs between us."

Gary looked speculatively at the jeep. "But we have two good legs," he
    said.
"Hunting season started at dawn,"
I said, knowing I wasn't saying anything.
"If we left now, we could get there a little after noon," Gary replied.

I reached for my crutches. He was holding his crutches.
Three minutes later we were in the jeep mimicking driving with two good
    legs.
I stepped on the clutch; Gary stepped on the gas.
We decided that if we had to stop quick, we'd let the engine die as I
    braked.

Thirty minutes later we were hauling happily out of Orchard Mesa
    toward Delta,
rifles in the back seat, and sure we were going to get a couple of bucks
even though climbing a hill was tantamount to ending up in the
    emergency room.

At Fool's Hill a coyote loped onto the road and stopped, looking at the
     jeep.
As I swerved, Gary took his foot off the gas and touched the brake.
We swung around yellow eyes sweet as you please.
Neither of us could stop congratulating each other on our driving skill.
.

By the time we'd come to the Paonia turnoff, we were tired,
and I was wondering what we thought we were doing.
Neither of us had been out of the hospital a week,
and the kitchen table note we'd left
was bound to get mom so agitated dad would be in the Ford
driving like a mad man toward where we said we were going.
Gary was manic, though. Hunting season was open.

From Paonia we climbed into the hills on a boulder filled dirt track.
Three miles from pavement we pulled into a meadow exhausted.
Clutching, shifting, leg-reaching, hand and arm coordination wasn't
     working.
The jeep stopped, we sat in our seats
and stared at country five miles from where our note said we'd be.
Where we were was a nightmare for two boys
who hadn't figured out how to carry rifles across uneven ground on
     crutches.

After a minute Gary said, "Looks like good deer country to me,"
and he was out of the jeep, figuring out how he was going to carry his
     30.06.
Back home we'd managed by pressing gun butt against crutch
and slowly making our way to the jeep.
But we couldn't hold gun and crutches tight while climbing.
At last Gary unbuckled his belt and tied the rifle to his crutch.

An hour later, hurting so bad neither of us could stand the pain,
we had climbed our first hill and were staring at a small wash
snaked through twisted slopes, a rock and brush nightmare.
I sat down and looked at anguish on Gary's face.
Why had I been so eager to go along with a fool idea?
Wasn't I the oldest? Shouldn't I have been the one with good sense?

Gary's face lit up. He grinned as if he'd hit the world's biggest jackpot.
He bent to unstrap the 30.06 from his crutch.

A two-point buck stood in the scrub oak wash below us.

I wasn't prepared for the shot when Gary fired.
I slid off the sloping rock where I was sitting and found myself
with my leg higher than my head with no idea how to leverage myself
to an upright position on the rock.

Gary started shouting, a mad man: "I got it!" he yelled. "I got it!"

He'd shot the buck? Thought dimly forced through my dilemma.
How were we going to get the buck, rifles,
and ourselves out of the wash, up the hill, down the hill,
and into the jeep so we could drive home?
How were we going to drive home when we were both on our last legs?

I stared at Gary, watched him hobble a victory dance,
and thought, "Damned you've been stupid, Tom."
Then, leg throbbing and burning up in my cast,
I maneuvered to my feet.

"Come on, Tommy," Gary said.
"Let's get this sucker and go out and get you one!"
I stared at my brother. Who was he anyway?
"How are we going to carry a buck out of here?" I asked.

Gary looked at me. "We'll drag it," he said.
"Won't do the hide any good,
but I got my buck first day of hunting season."

"Have you figured out how we're going to get into the wash?" I asked.
"Why should I worry about that?" Gary shot back, puzzled.
"We just get down there, put a rope around the buck, and drag it out."

"Your foot hurt?" I asked.
He shot me a look of pure malice.
"Of course, my foot hurts," he snarled. "So does your leg."
He looked at the sky.
"Sunset will be here before we get back to the jeep."
I didn't say anything but put crutches beneath arm pits.

Once we got into the wash, I strained to hold dead weight high enough
for Gary to rope the buck's neck.

Gary tied the rope around his waist
and started making his way up the hill.

An hour and a half later, sun going down,
I had the rope around my waist. Gary wasn't talking anymore.
I'd suggested we give up and leave the buck for later,
but he'd gotten so upset I thought he was going to hit me,
so we struggled, fighting uphill until we saw the jeep.
Then I carefully put crutches downhill as far as I dared,
planted points into ground and dragged downward,
cussing silently at pain, my idiocy, and my stupid, stupid brother.

When dad finally came up the dirt road, headlights on,
he climbed the hill, took one look at Gary, then me,
then the buck, then shook his head.

Without another word he untied the rope from my waist,
grabbed the buck's horns and pulled it toward the jeep.
At the jeep, catching his breath, he said,
"We'll take the car home. We'll get the jeep tomorrow."
A warning was in his voice:
"Mom will have to drive home from here."

Gary fell asleep before we'd gotten off the dirt road.
Dad winced every time the car crept over a boulder and scraped its frame.
He kept silent so long I couldn't stand silence any longer.

"I was a damned fool," I said at last.
"I shouldn't have gotten us in this mess."

Dad didn't say anything for a long time.
 "At least you left a note," he said at last.
"A wise man always leaves a note."

We turned off the dirt road toward Paonia.
I squirmed and wondered how Gary could sleep through his pain.
In the hospital I'd heard him screaming half the night.
Then the car tire's humming weighed down eyelids, and I fell asleep,
knowing a man ought to do more than "leave a note" in life.

Up Jacob's Ladder

We broke into the cabin beneath the canyon's sandstone wall.
Howard dug in deep snow, found a rock, and tapped
until he'd chiseled a jagged hole in the windowpane.
Then he stuck his coat-protected arm inside,
pulled the latch and, smiling, opened the pine door.

We had started out that morning at 5:00 a.m.
and climbed Jacob's Ladder in the dark
until we were above scattered houses,
traveling on gravel roads as the sun's red edge
trembled on Grand Mesa's horizon.
We were exhilarated to be free from town
on the Uncompahgre Plateau climbing to high country.
December's heavy snows weighed tree branches down,
but we were in a power wagon and could plow through
any amount of snow we found in our way.
Our goal was to find the best pine and spruce Christmas trees
growing in Colorado so we could sell them
outside my father's small supermarket on Orchard Mesa
and be flush with cash for the holidays.

By 2:00 p.m. we'd left pinyon and juniper forests behind
and climbed into aspen, spruce, ponderosa pine, and pine.
We were bucking snow up to the power wagon's front bumper
when Howard pulled to a stop and announced
we'd found Christmas Tree heaven.
Minutes later we'd grabbed axes from the wagon's truck bed
and were in the trees, sending chips flying.
Two hours later the truck bed was full,
day was falling, and my recently operated-on knee was throbbing.

When the power wagon started and the heater kicked in,
I leaned back in my seat and breathed relief.
We started chugging back down the mountain toward home.
Twenty minutes later, still a half mile from the dirt road,
we lurched to a halt, steam rising from the hood in fading light.

"Damned," Howard said, then got out of the driver's seat,
popped the cab's green hood and fumbled around the engine block.

I sat in gathering cold and waited, hoping and holding my breath.
The nearest house was fifteen miles away.
In too short a time Howard had the hood closed,
and he was looking at me with almost-angry intensity.

"If I had a girlfriend, we'd be all right." He threw the words at me.
"I'd have pantyhose in the cab. They'd work for a fan belt.
Nothing's stronger than pantyhose.
They could get us off this damned mountain."

I just looked at him. The fan belt was broke? We couldn't drive any
        further?
Fluorescent light surrounding ceiling tiles above my hospital bed
flickered as the nurse wrapped a cast's clammy warmth around my leg.
I hadn't been out of that cast for two weeks yet.

Had I ever really felt fear before? I asked myself,
looking at Howard and the spindly mustache
he'd started growing a month before.
Was I afraid now?

"We'd better start walking then," I said quietly.
Howard nodded, but didn't say anything else.

I hadn't felt the cold all day. I'd swung an axe and moved around
and kept myself so warm I'd taken off my coat, sweating.
Now, moving steadily behind Howard in tire tracks we'd made earlier,
I couldn't get my mind off the cold. I stared at ground
and wondered how I'd been stupid enough to go along on this adventure.
Couldn't I learn that Howard didn't have a healthy sense of fear?

Darkness settled; the winter moon, small, hard, and white, rose.
We came to the graveled road. I was feeling pretty good.
My leg was hurting, but I was handling the pain,
and though Howard was moving faster than I was
and had to stop to wait off and on, I was still making pretty good time.
Then we came to a steep hill rutted into a dry gulch.
Three-quarters of the way down my bad leg gave way,
and I fell, sliding hard on frozen ground.

"Tommy!" Howard said, coming back to help me get up.
"You alright?" He paused, looking concerned.

"We can't stop. Not any time soon."
I didn't look at him. I wasn't even eighteen, I thought to myself.
I wasn't even eighteen.

I shrugged Howard off and started walking down the road.
Leg, I told myself. You've got to do better than that.

Not much further, and I had fallen again,
and Howard was hovering over me again.
I got up and walked until I fell again. Then, after another fall,
I rubbed bare fingers together inside my coat pocket.
They were numb. I brought my hand out into moonlight.

"I've lost a glove," I said to myself.

Howard, two steps ahead, stopped.
"What?" he asked, his voice apprehensive.
"My right-hand glove is gone," I said.

He looked at me as if he couldn't understand what I was telling him.
"It'll get below zero before daybreak," he said quietly. "Below zero."

I didn't look at him but started walking again.
Mind numb as my fingers, I shoved fingers back into my pocket.

Howard stood looking at me. I felt his eyes on my back.
"Damned," he said. "Damned."
Then he was ahead of me again.

The next time I fell I tried to keep my hand in my pocket,
but pulled it out to keep from slamming face first into the ground.

"Come on leg," I said out-loud.
The scar over my kneecap burned pain.
"You can't give up now."

I wouldn't let Howard touch me,
but struggled to my feet and forced myself to limp forward.
"Pain is nothing," I said out loud, half shouting.
"Come on leg, we've got to move!"

Howard didn't say anything or even look at me,

but pushed further and further ahead.
I fell again and again, and every time I scrambled up
and closed my mind to leg fire and numb fingers
until, finally, Howard had stopped at a fork in the road and was waiting.

"We've found it," he said. "Found what?" I asked.

Howard pointed at the south fork that led back up the mountain.
"There's a cabin up here," he said. "I remember a cabin up here."

I looked at the road that led toward Jacob's Ladder.
I thought about how I'd climbed and climbed and found heaven
And how heaven had frost bit my fingers and made my leg hurt.

"If you're wrong, we'll have to walk even further," I said.
I unconsciously touched my bad leg.

Howard stared and stared at the south road
and felt an eternity of stars above our heads.
He didn't answer my unspoken question,
but left the road we'd been following and started climbing.

"Come on leg," I said. "We can't be alone together."

The road went on and on and on into moon-stained cold.
Walking toward the cabin, keeping myself on my feet without falling,
I realized I'd left my sick fear back on the Jacob's Ladder Road.
If the cabin wasn't there, it wasn't there.
We'd turn around and walk toward Jacob's Ladder again.
Neither my leg, fingers, me, or Howard would give up and die.

But then the cabin was there, small and isolated in the dark.

"I told you," Howard said, looking at the window over the doorknob.

"We can't break in," I said without thinking. "We don't know who the
     owner is."

Howard looked at me, an incredulous look on his face, and shook his
     head.
"My God, Tommy," he said. "You really are a character."
Then he dug a hand-sized stone out of the snow behind us.

Our first stop inside was the kitchen where we found stale crackers
that tasted like manna must have tasted to the Hebrews
starving in their search for the promised land.
Then we found two down sleeping bags and bunk beds.
"I'll take the top bunk," Howard said, lifting himself off the floor.

I crawled into the sleeping bag I was borrowing for the night
and closed my eyes, falling asleep before I realized
my fingers were hurting nearly as badly as my leg was.

I didn't dream but slept toward the man I would become.

Prophecy

We were picnicking in Cactus Park above Nine Mile Hill.
My Uncle JT, Aunt Viola, Uncle David, Aunt Stella, mom, dad, brothers,
    and cousins
played horseshoes, softball, and put plates of food on homemade quilts.
I was looking at dry, reddish soils when I found petrified dinosaur bone.
Then I saw sandstone chippings where arrowheads might be found.

For a time, I heard Davises, Jacks, and Morrises at play.
Then I lost those sounds without realizing they were gone.
One chipping pile led to another to another.
Hungry, I looked up from ground.
The high desert was silent with old silence.

I slowly turned a circle, listening.
Wind blew through sage.
I didn't panic but walked back the way I had come.
I could still see faint footsteps in soil on sandstone.
I lost the tracks, stopped, looked up.

The universe pooled outward, rising into sky eternities.
I disappeared into wind, trees, sandstone, sand, cactus, sage, raven cries.
Fear dried my throat.
I walked toward a ridge not far from where I was.
If I climbed high enough, I would see the picnic. I'd be okay.

Early afternoon heat prickled skin sweat.
An hour later I looked across Cactus Park.
I could see no sign of family or picnic, only the high desert valley's sweep.

Exhausted, I sat against a crooked pinion tree's trunk.
Heat wavered. Intent, lost in musing, half asleep, afraid…

Time, disjointed, danced.
An old man, dressed in deer skins, skin leathery brown,
stopped as he climbed the ridge and looked at me.
Men, women, and children circled a campfire dancing.
Wolves and coyotes sang to night inside noonday's heat.

My mom looked at my dad and said, "He's lost."

My dad shook his head. "No," he said. "He's a Colorado boy."
"You'll have to go find him," my mom answered.

Red and black horses galloped, tails flying, then disappeared.

I slept beneath branches crooked out of a gnarled trunk.
I saw myself sleeping in the tree's shade, face untroubled.

Juniper and pinyon forests withered.
Needles browned, dropped from brittle branches.
In distant oceans cold water glaciers drowned the Gulf Stream.
Severe sunlight beat down. Rain stopped falling.
The Unaweep Canyon stream flowing to the Gunnison River disappeared.
Sun shimmered water hallucinations.
Great fires towered black smoke and leaping, fulminating flames.
Coyotes abandoned the plateau and loped, tongues hanging, to search for water.
On Grand Mesa's blue distance lakes dried into cracked mud.
Lakebeds lost even the cracks and filled with dry rye grasses.
Hot winds blew wretchedness into whirling dust devils.

A blue jay darted from a branch above my head.
I woke and moved to the ridge rim.
I saw my dad, uncle, and brothers and took off running downhill.
My dad saw me and started running.
I shouted. He shouted. My brothers and uncle shouted.
A half hour later relatives surrounded me,
hugging, chewing me out, laughing,
and I was a part of them …

Dust devils dance out of gluttonous walls of cavorting flames.

David Winger and I sat on a foothill looking out

over the Gunnison River in the middle of the night.

We were sixteen, and the Milky Way was a smear of light
echoing into unimaginable distances
that seemed to us, sitting there, and looking up,
as if they were a music pulsing with light, darkness,
and our own heartbeats as we tried to imagine
who we were inside immensity.

"Maybe we're on an atom beside a billion other atoms
whirling so fast in time they form the substance
that is another atom in another universe
that leads to other atoms in other universes," I said.

"Maybe there's a world where our universe is flotsam
sailing down a rushing stream
being looked at by two guys bigger than our universe
trying to figure out why they feel so small," David answered.

And above our heads, as time passed in that night
when he and I were still so young,
the light of stars flowed through solar winds
from a billion shining silver stars that were suns.
Time wove with layers of our ancestors who had died
and our descendants who were not yet born
and all the animals and plants that had ever lived and died
and the coalescing inside fires of star nurseries
birthing stars that will one day blaze into novae
dying into black holes centering universes.

Our spirits sailed, meaning we still weren't sure who we were
on the third planet from the sun
in the foothills of a valley shining beneath light
from silver stars on a moonless night.

Library in the Canyon

We saw the old man sometimes when we fished riverbanks
west of Orchard Mesa dump in the canyon.
We were afraid of him and held our breaths
as he walked along railroad tracks beside the Gunnison.
He was unremarkable to look at, disheveled and thin.
He lived in a shack he'd built with stacked stones and a tin roof
receded into red sandstone.
The shack couldn't be seen from railroad tracks or canyon rim,
but only if you were looking for a slanting slit
angled northwest into the canyon wall.

A half mile from the shack two gray metal shelves had been placed
beneath a rock overhang and filled with old books, mostly classics:
Dumas, Fox Jr., Kipling, Stevenson, Boyd, Cervantes, Twain …
I never knew if the old man made the library,
though I suspected he had and sometimes thought
I would get brave and see if he liked to read.

Back home, away from the canyon, I dreamed
about taking some of my favorite hard cover editions
and adding them to the small collection I was beginning to build,
but I never did, though I never saw anyone visit the books.
They never changed in title or number from season to season.

I only visited the canyon library when I was alone.
The only bookworm I knew, I was afraid that if my friends found the
    books
they would have a great time throwing them in the river.
Sometimes I would borrow a book during long summer days
and spend hours reading on a giant boulder
protruded from sand banks into river current.
Sitting on the rock in summer light beneath a Colorado sky,
whiling away hours lost in ancient England as knights
clashed in desperate battles that would decide the fate of nations,
I felt past and present universes breathe.

I always returned the book, dust and dirt stains half removed,
placing it back in the exact spot from which I had taken it.

I hadn't visited the secret library in a while.
I was digging fossils out of the shale arroyos
not far from where the Gunnison and canyon curved
toward its grand junction with the Colorado River.
In the ancient fossil library's dimness,
looking at the skeleton of a tiny ancient fish,
I got to thinking about the library beneath the rock overhang.
I left the arroyo and headed for the canyon.
When I got to where the library should have been,
gray shelves and books were gone.

I stood in sunshine beneath blue sky and felt loss and betrayal.
How could something that wonderful be gone?
I should have talked to the old man at least once, I thought.
I should have found out if reading lessened his loneliness.

As soon as I thought about the old man
I walked railroad tracks to the old man's hidden shack,
but all that was left were the front wall's stacked stones.
Confused, I walked up to the filthy blanket door
and went into the crack that had once been a man's home.
Dirt had been leveled to make a floor,
but nothing else was there—no tin roof, bed, table, chair, or books.

I walked to where I'd spent hours
reading books from a library that no longer existed.
I sat on the great boulder and listened to lapping water
and felt the shared humanity of words conjured
from the dust of a library of old books kept by an old man
who lived in a handmade shack not far from the town dump.

The Storm

Lightning lit foothills alive in great off and on flashes over and over.
Blue-white traceries forked sustained fury into darkness.
Pinyon trees, rocks, and gullies danced white, hot light in the night:
Wind, thunder, rain, dry gullies filled with floods heard but not seen.

I was alone in Malone Cave below the crest of a hill littered with
    sandstone slabs.
I was there because when my parents had decided to visit the
    Manspeakers,
and I had wanted to go off with Larry Vertree and other friends,
I had suddenly blown up, blood boiling rage, and walked into the hills.
My dad had watched me go, shaking his head, but hadn't tried to stop
    me.
The strange thing was that I really liked the Manspeakers.
My brothers and I had grown up with them and their friendship.

Now I was in the cave looking out at a landscape bizarre with fury.
I should have been safe, but a leak had slowly widened to an expanding
    stream
where the cave's sandstone roof embedded into hill.

Then a big cat snarled in the dark, wind, and rain.
A mountain lion! I thought. I've never heard of a mountain lion in the
    foothills!
I looked at a landscape shadowed by lightning flashes, straining to see
    the lion,
but there was nothing, only hillsides alive with rivulets of rainwater.
I couldn't stay still. What would my parents, my brothers, be thinking?
Would the mountain lion decide it needed the cave more
than a teenage boy who had ridden storm winds
into a mess he wasn't prepared to face?

Suddenly, without deciding, I was out of the cave.
Rain was cold, plastering shirt to skin.
The world smelled wet, sizzled with lightning-ozone.
As I walked, half-slid through mud that covered new shoes,
I entered another universe where rolling black clouds, thunder, gusting
    wind, water raging in dry gullies, mountain lions enraged by the
    smell of wet fur

sucked up time and made it disappear into an uncontrolled universe's
    reality.
I came to a small gully and roaring whitewater and hesitated,
watching as current ate into the bank's rim like a ravenous snake.
Why had I left the cave for the night's insane chaos?
The question repeated and repeated itself in my head.
I plunged into the gully's torrent and staggered from the water's force.
Panicked, I drove myself forward into water up to my waist.
Was I going to die before I even had a steady girlfriend?

I fell forward onto the gully's opposite bank and crawled in mud to
    higher ground.
Rain kept falling and falling.
Lightning jagged, danced, lit rain slants falling.
Lost in nightmare, mindlessly moving,
I was swallowed by sky-earth-storm.

I crossed another raging gully, then another.
Then I was climbing the face of hills before the irrigation canal
just before Orchard Mesa's north-of-Highway-51 neighborhoods.

At the canal's bank I stopped.
All of us kids had learned how to jump from one bank to another.
We couldn't get wet and let our parents know we'd been to the foothills
and the start of wilderness that rose into the Uncompahgre Plateau.
Every chance we got we jumped the canal, climbed hills, then started
    walking to sandstone squeezers, Malone's Cave, fossil fissures,
    Gunnison River canyon, railroad tracks inside the canyon, sloughs
    and sandbars where you could fish or see mallards glistening in
    summer sun.

But now I stood on the west bank and felt as if I weighed a thousand
    pounds.
My shoes were caked mud, my shirt and blue jeans waterlogged, heavy.
There were fools, and then there was me, I told myself.
I backed up and tried to run through the mud and jumped.
For a second my head was underwater as I grabbed at the bank.
The water was too swift to stand up in, but somehow, I clambered,
one leg at a time, out of the ditch. I couldn't stop shivering.
My breath came in huge, panicked gulps.
My head swam with emptiness larger than the storm.

When I walked past the darkened Manspeaker house,
I told myself over and over again, just keep moving, just keep moving.
I had passed into insanity, I told myself.
To be safe all I had to do was to keep telling myself to keep moving.

At last, I crossed an empty Highway 51, climbed down the hill with two
     apricot trees, and stood in front of my house.
The lights were still on.
I could see my mother looking out, but not seeing me in the dark.
How in the world could I go inside and face my family?
Thunder rolled and rolled into flash after flash of lightning as rain fell
     and fell.

Then, miraculously, I was out of the rain inside in my bed,
my father's and mother's worried faces above me.
They kept telling me that everything was going to be all right.
I couldn't stop shaking. I mumbled words I knew made no sense over
     and over.
We'll take care of this, my dad said. You're here; you'll be okay, my
     mom said.
But inside the storm of myself I was wondering, could I ever be okay?
or would I always suddenly find myself in a storm of my own making,
struggling toward a safety madness would force me to deny?

Christmas Day: Sledding on the Mountain

We drove Grand Mesa's unpaved, snow-packed roads
around hairpin curves until the banks
of drifts were high enough to stop the plows.
Grandparents, uncles, aunts, and cousins slammed
car doors and shouted so their voices echoed off
the slopes and cliffs that soared into the sky.
Then "food enough to feed an army," sleds,
toboggans came from car trunks as the day's
festivity spilled out into the winter cold.
My dad and uncle dug into the snow
to make a fire with driftwood, branches found
down in the canyon as we'd driven by
the stream that gurgled songs beneath the ice.

Then, looking down the road toward a bank
that lurched uphill before a hairpin curve,
the oldest of my cousins laughed and jumped
onto her sled, her head downhill, and slid
like lightning flashed into a coal-black sky:
The slope so steep she flew, the hill of white
a half mile down as solid as a wall,
the road beneath her hard and slick as ice.

Her mother, Aunt Viola, laughed to see
her fly toward the snowbank wall as I
could hardly breathe to see the tragedy
unfolding as the sunlight glared into my eyes.
My eyes began to hurt. She had to crash
or slam into the wall of snow so hard
she wouldn't be my cousin anymore.

But, as she hurtled down toward her doom,
she dragged her legs behind the racing sled
and turned the blades before she hit the hill,
and everybody who had stopped to watch
began to yell when she rolled off the sled,
popped to her feet and shot her arm into the air.

When, after other cousins dared the hill,
I hesitated, swallowing to see
the downhill slope, my younger brother jumped
ahead of me and joined in the fun.
I stood above my sled and felt my heart
quail, staring down toward the distant bank
that still seemed solid as a concrete wall.

I froze and couldn't move until my dad,
behind me, got me on my sled and pushed
me off as cold and snow and light became
a blur of flying, flying down the road.
I flared my legs behind the hurtling sled
and tried to slow down as I turned the blades,
the running sound beneath my stomach, snow
a cloud of ice as I rolled off the sled
and came up, sunk in snow up to my hips,
and shouted with my arm up in the air.

The Light

The night breathed sounds and darkness.
The earth was warm,
and the crickets—I think they were crickets—
maybe frogs were in the music too—
sang beneath stars luminous across sky.

Beneath us the canyon yawned
with a darkness more intense
than that covering pinion and juniper around us,
sandstone of rimrock
stretching in a horseshoe
from where we stood
into hills we knew were there
but could not see.
The air had a fresh smell,
as if rain was coming
even though the sky was filled with stars.

Then silence. No wind. No cricket songs. Silence.

Floating out of sky
so slowly you could just barely see
its sliding sideways, pulsing movement,
a glaring ball of light
lit up night,
elongating shadows
and dimming the Milky Way's river of light,
electrifying air
as if suddenly the world was overcharged
and spilling out of itself into sky.
Trees about us danced with shadows
that a moment before were not there.
Silence roared at us
as we glanced away from light
at the suddenly rusty color of canyon walls
and looked at the fierce ball
no longer falling,
but moving down and up and sideways
one way and then another.

"Would you look at that?" Jim said.
"An unidentified flying object."

We watched until it disappeared,
and midnight had come and gone,
and stars and canyon night sounds
had come back into the world.

Then we drove down curvy mountain roads
back to Grand Junction,
looking at the city
gleaming in a carpet of distant light
as we fell from the mountain
until finally we were away from the canyon,
excited,
eating cherry and pecan pie
in the wee hours of morning.

The Meaning of Human Time

Bill Johnson called out, "An arrowhead! A beaut!"
and the Grand Junction Izaac Walton Club
broke the hunting line walking across sagebrush flats
and rushed to a small mesa.
We put down twenty-twos and four-tens
and started hunting arrowheads, seven pairs of eyes
eager to find sandstone or flint shaped into points
by skill and craft of ancient hands.

We had crossed into Utah from Colorado west of Mack
earlier that morning, filled with exuberance.
We turned toward alluvial dirt fans of Bookcliff mountains
and drove until we couldn't hear the Interstate,
and then got down to the serious business of hunting.

We hadn't shot a single jack rabbit when Bill found his mesa.
From then on through a hot day jack rabbits were safe.
We plunged into circles of flaked sandstone where Anasazi
had spent patient hours applying pressure and chipping stone.

By noon we'd found over a hundred and twenty arrowheads.
Some were finished and elegantly shaped,
points sweeping back with smooth, shallow indentations
to where growing width triangled and abruptly hollowed, curved
into the small flare where the head was set into the arrow shaft.
Some were rougher, ill or half made,
as if the maker had been rushed and hadn't had time
to fashion art that would last the ages on a small mesa.
By the time a purple and pink sunset fired the western horizon,
we'd found over two hundred arrowheads.
We were so wild with discovery we were prepared to stay all night
        searching.

In the desert's evening cool,
David Winger, who loved to speculate about the universe,
built a fire on the mesa's low end
where we hadn't found knapping circles or arrowheads.
As darkness gathered, one after another shambled
to the fire and found a place.

No moon rose, so even the mesa disappeared into dark intensity.
"Why do you figure they made so many arrowheads here?"
David asked after we were around his fire.

"Had to provide defense for a city in the Bookcliffs," Bill answered.

"The Bookcliffs are pretty far away from here," Richard Shelly said.
"Must be another four- or five-mile hike at least."

"But this is the highest point around here," Bill pointed out.
"The Old Ones could have seen anything coming.
Maybe runners warned the city if they spotted trouble."

"I've never heard of Anasazi in the Bookcliffs," I said.

David's face brooded behind thick rimmed glasses.

"Bill's right," he said. "If we walked straight north of here
into the canyon that opens out of the Bookcliff's face
and spent the time, we'd eventually find where Old Ones lived."

"It's spooky," Sandy Dallas said. "You can almost feel
the people who made the arrowheads walking around."

A couple of guys laughed; nervousness hidden by sound.

"I wonder what it means that we found this place?" David asked.
"I mean, why us? A bunch of regular high school guys from Grand
    Junction?"

"There's got to be a reason?" Richard asked.
"We wanted to go rabbit hunting. Bill had his eyes on the ground.
We found what we've found."

"You don't think Old Ones had anything to do with us being here?"
David asked. "Sandy's right. They're here right now.
Not here *here*, but in the sense, they spent decades
making knapping circles. Night after night. Day after day.
This is their place. Not ours. We're here because of them."

A coyote yipped darkness. Not the full-blown song
of coyotes singing a full moon, but a disturbance of silence.

We sat on the mesa in the aloneness that followed
and thought long thoughts that tried to bridge time.
We could almost see men who had sat watching from the mesa
defending mothers, fathers, wives, and children,
looking to horizons for whatever danger they feared.
In the campfire's circle we felt so close as human beings,
we seemed as if we would never break apart
even though we all knew that after high school,
we would scatter and follow paths that led to who knew where?

I look back on that day and night as an aging man.
Most of the Grand Junction Izaak Walton Club of 1964
have disappeared into their lives.
Bill Johnson's dad left his mom, and Bill became Paul Pletka, a famous
    artist.
Richard Shelly was drafted, went to Viet Nam, and died.
David Winger went to work as a ranger in Eastern Colorado.
The arrowheads were given to a Utah Museum
and the mesa shown to archeologists.
I never heard if they discovered a Bookcliff Anasazi cliff dwelling.

Yet, on that hill, in the circle of campfire ashes long gone,
the Izaak Walton Club is still there,
along with Old Ones, men, women, and children
who once stared long at the Utah desert's vast sweep.
David Winger's campfire still burns small in a night with no moon.
A coyote still yips in an immense night,
and jackrabbits live lives as if hunters do not exist,
and the mesa is a place that has never been visited by humankind.

Paul Gallico's *The Snow Goose*

Books and manuscripts piled to the ceiling on golden maple
     bookshelves attached to all four walls,
eyes shining behind gold rimmed glasses,
the old woman, sherry in hand, sat behind a round table
dancing with men and women tumbling in air over sharp horns of great
     bulls
drawn with colorful tiles snipped, cut, and placed into life's movement.

"Edward Abby doesn't have anything on T.E. Lawrence," she was
     saying.
"Lawrence was an old-fashioned scholar-hero who got out of his easy
     chair
and learned the desert on a camel's back and by sleeping in a tent.
In Moab, Abby climbs red rocks and finds a mule in a dry canyon
     during a rainstorm
and comes to conclusions not driven by the storm of being."

In the living room Bill Johnson, who will become Paul Pletka[1],
is painting a Christmas scene on the door's leaded window,
making sure each brush stroke is as precise as the ticking of an
     expensive clock.
A rabbit, sitting in snow beside a gully choked with snow-burdened
     sagebrush,
bristled life in the night beneath the Christmas star's shining silver.

How did I rate being there in that magnificent old house? I thought to
     myself.
I remembered how my English teacher in 10th grade,
discovering I was reading Dostoevsky's *Crime and Punishment* in the
     school's library,
sneered, commenting softly that he thought I was not ready for so
     heavy a novel.

Mildred Hart Shaw sipped on dark ruby-red sherry and looked at me.
She pulled a clipping from the *Daily Sentinel* out of the blue, green, and
     white plaid jacket she was wearing
and handed it to me.

---

[1] Paul has become one of the premier Western artists in the United States

"You know," she said. "I've been doing book reviews for thirty years,
and I've never gotten a fan letter once." She smiled.
I looked at the letter addressed to Thomas Davis c/o the *Daily Sentinel*,
     Grand Junction, Colorado.
It was from a woman who lived in Delta, the town where I was born.
It burned in my hand.

Bill, paint splotched on the back of his left hand,
came from the living room and stood in the library's dark oak arch.
He was smiling like Mildred was smiling.

"I always knew you'd make it as a poet, Tommy," he said.

"The book review was prose," I mumbled softly, surprised I'd spoken.
"No, you're a poet," Mildred answered, finality in her voice.
"I can just barely get Keats," I said. "If I work at it."

"I'm done with the window," Bill who would become Paul said.

Mildred's smile was as bright as the shining in her eyes.
"Wonderful," she said. "This is turning out to be a good Christmas."

I thought of the disappointment I'd felt
when my grades were too low to be eligible to join Great Books
     evenings
Mildred Hart Shaw held with honors high school students
at her house down the street from Mesa College's campus
and thought about the hours I'd spent
wallowing in the emotional pain of a back growing humped
because of a disease growing from genes
echoing backward into generations I knew nothing about.

"We need a good out-loud read," Mildred said. "We'll take turns."

She pulled a slender orange, hardbound copy of Paul Gallico's *The Snow
     Goose*
from crowded shelves without thinking about where the volume was
     sitting.

"You first, Tommy," she said. "You got the fan letter."
She looked at Bill. "Though you're going to be famous," she said.
Bill smiled, delighted at the thought.

"The marsh lies on the Essex Coast between the village of Chelmbury
   and the ancient Saxon oyster-fishing hamlet of Wickaeldroth," I
   read,

and the day's magic gathered into words dancing and singing
into symphonies of forever.

Genius: Mildred and Bill

A sherry in her hand, surrounded by
the books that filled the room from floor to ceiling,
she watched the young man, self-absorbed, apply
a tiny brush to lead-framed glass, a feeling
of richness emanating from a scene
of large-eared rabbits sitting in the snow
beside a gully, mountains rising white, pristine,
into a winter sky that almost glowed.

The glass had traveled west a hundred years ago
strapped in a wagon pulled by two huge horses.
"That's good," she said. "It has a Christmas glow.
No rivers, but it sets the rivers in their courses."

"A Christmas door," he said. "It's here, but then
you'll wipe it clean to make it just a door again."

What Happens When You Get Old

Afraid, Grandma started talking
about the two weeping willows in her back yard.
When the wind blows, they move around
and make complaining noises, she said.
She said she was waking up late at night
and hearing them in the dark.

In her early seventies she still loved
gardening and growing flowers.
Her row of red and pink peonies
beside her driveway's black cinders,
usually covered with crawling ants,
bloomed all spring and summer.
After she and Grandpa George had built their adobe house
putting earth-bricks together by hand,
she'd planted climbing rose bushes,
creating a rose arch in front of the front door.

Later, behind the willows she'd planted
after snipping twigs off a massive tree
growing beside her favorite fishing hole
at Schweitzer Lake and sprouting white roots in a glass jar,
she started a garden with concord grape vines,
strawberries, sweet corn, sugar beets, potatoes, lettuce,
green beans, and tomatoes bigger than tomatoes ought to be.
During late fall days, before the cold came,
she spent hours, florid face red and sweating,
putting the year's harvest in mason jars.

When she finally let the garden go
after getting a job at Goodwill downtown,
the willows started worrying her.
She complained about them as if she thought
they were angry at her the way her neighbor was.

He claimed that when she and George
had built their house in the poor part of Delta
they'd put their porch and cellar
six inches into land he had purchased a decade later.

Finally, one night when she couldn't sleep,
she went out and tried to chop the tallest willow down
with a rusty axe from the coal shed.
When she discovered she'd grown too old
to manage that in the middle of the night,
she called an old man she'd known for sixty years
and had him chop down both willows
"For firewood to feed his wood stove."

In a Delta, Colorado Nursing Home

My aging aunt put her hand on my shoulder.
"Talk to her, Tommy," she told me.
"We know she hears us.
She moves her head while we're talking."

Grandma Davis was comatose,
chin skin flaccid; her face, once dark-skinned,
now blanched, absence in her dark eyes.

I glanced at my aunt and wondered
what in the world she expected me to say?

"Dad told me you were in trouble,
to get to Uncle David's fast," I whispered at last.
"I drove like a maniac,
ninety miles an hour down that two-lane road.
I was scared I was going to kill somebody."

I paused.

"I kept thinking of my Grandfather George,"
I told her. "How Grandmother Bauer
left us three boys alone with him
a couple of days before he died.
He was propped up in bed
and glanced at us staring at him.
He whispered, 'hello boys.'

They didn't let us go to the funeral . . ."

My voice tailed off.
My aunt touched my shoulder again.

"She can hear us," my aunt soft softy.
"That's important."

On the Road to Perdition

1

I didn't know what time it was when my mom's voice woke me.
She sounded angry.
Then I heard my brother slurring his words, cussing at her.
I'd just gotten into the hallway outside my room
when I saw my dad looking bleary-eyed behind my mother
as she confronted my equally angry brother
as he waved his arms in the air.
"Bitch!" my brother spit into the dark.

I didn't see my dad move.
Suddenly my mom was behind him as he punched
and knocked my brother on his ass.
Gary was crying as he looked up at my dad bent over him,
telling him he'd never disrespect his mother that way again.

My dad didn't even yell at us boys.
What was going on?
I heard a noise behind me and saw my little brother
coming from where he and Gary shared a room,
his eyes the size of saucers.

2

At five a.m.,
just before my dad usually got up to open the store,
a sheriff's deputy knocked on the kitchen door.

"I've got to arrest Gary," he told my dad
who had come out of his bedroom still in his undershirt.
"He and his buddies collapsed the evangelist preacher's tent,
destroying the old man's piano."

Rattler

They'd been drinking. Eyes shined, and they were excited.
They had been by the Colorado River in Utah canyon fishing,
catching mostly catfish, but occasionally a sucker, bonehead, bass, or
    trout,
and were halfway up the dirt road's outcroppings of boulders
when they spotted a diamondback rattlesnake six feet long
and thicker than an old apple tree's trunk.
They stopped the rusted-out pickup and got out,
carefully avoiding the big rattler, its rattling warning of quickness and
    poison.
My brother found a forked stick from a cottonwood lying beside the
    road
even though the nearest river-cottonwoods were miles away
and got more excited.

"Look at this!" he said, waving the stick in the air,
not taking his eyes off the rattler.

 "You're nuts, Gary," Darrell said. "Or too drunk to know better."
He laughed, sounding nervous.

"I can barely walk," Gary said. "But I'm faster than anybody."
"Leave that snake alone," Darrell warned.

Gary smiled, dark, sun-weathered skin contrasting with his eyes'
    brightness.
"Watch," he said, eyes drilling into the snake's long, flickering tongue.
The snake concentrated on him, impersonally malevolent,
head as still and tense as unblinking eyes.

Gary didn't think about consequences that had flowed
from when he, Darrell, and his other buddies
had decided to cut ropes used to keep a show preacher's revival tent
    upright
and collapsed the whole thing at midnight,
unaware the revival organist was sleeping inside.
He was in the desert, away from civilization, in wilderness God had
    made.

Darrell watched, mouth open, as Gary inched toward the snake,
forked stick held like a spear in his right hand.
The rattler imperceptibly pulled back its head.
Its tongue stopped flickering.
Gary inched closer.
The snake coiled.
Gary struck, the stick flying toward the snake.
The great rattler writhed and twisted,
head caught inside the stick's fork.
Gary crowed like a rooster, triumphant, wild
even though he was gripping the stick so hard his knuckles were white.
Sweat poured down his face.

Darrell shook his head, comprehension eluding him.
"You captured a rattler," he said, the tone in his voice denying what
    he'd said.

Gary's eyes shined and danced with his excitement.
"Get the camera," he said. "It's in the front glove compartment."
"Gary?" Darrell asked.
"The camera, dammit," Gary said, insistent. "Hurry."

"What are you thinking?" Darrell asked. "I've seen that look before."
"The camera," Gary demanded.

Darrell took his eyes off Gary and the snake,
turned, opened the passenger-side door, and fumbled with the truck's
    glove compartment.
He shut the door behind him, focusing back on the rattler, camera in
    hand.
Gary grinned.

"Nobody'll believe us without proof," he said.

Then, as carefully as a diamond cutter chipping a facet into a diamond,
he moved toward the rattler.

"Gary," Darrell warned. "No."

Gary drilled his eyes at the snake's head caught in the stick's fork.
He knelt and moved close enough to the snake to touch cold, scaly
    skin.

Darrell held his breath.
Time stopped.
Even the ancient desert's long stillness of time stopped.
Gary bent over the snake's huge girth, its undulating body, and grabbed
the spot between the stick and its head,
standing up as the stick dropped to the ground.

"The photo," Gary demanded, his voice strained. "Now!"

The rattler hissed and writhed, trying to coil around its adversary.
Its mouth, with gleaming teeth, opened so wide it seemed unhinged,
it's strength so great Gary's arm moved despite his enormous effort to
    keep the snake away from his body.
Darrell snapped one, two, three pictures.

"What in the hell are you going to do now?" he roared angrily.
"That's a poisonous diamondback in your hand!"

Gary walked to a sandstone ledge seven or eight feet away and stepped
    upward,
dragging the rattler's tail off the ground.
Angry rattling filled the universe.
Gary moved the rattler back and forth, back and forth;
its tail swung higher and higher into the sky.
Then,

as he swung one last time,
he let go as fangs struck air beside his hand, barely missing flesh.
The rattler hit sand and slithered from Gary and pickup
as if fleeing the fires and madness of Hell.

Gary's sun-red face was bleach-white beneath his tan.
Bent over, he was shaking all over.
"Man," he said.

Darrell, alcohol driven out of him, shook his head.
"You're crazy," he said. "You're plumb nuts."

"You get the photo of me holding the rattler?" Gary asked.

Darrell shook his head again.
"Give me the keys," he said. "We're getting out of here."

Gary grinned. "Naw," he said, straightening up. "I'm all right.
Even it'd bitten me I'd be all right.
I may be crippled, but I'm as tough a man as ever lived."

He smiled maniacally; smile as bright as the noontime desert sun.

The First Day of Falling in Love

The day was bright with the harsh Colorado sun when we climbed into your sister Lorraine's old car and drove for a picnic in Unaweep Canyon. After writing letters to each other for a year, we had finally met after you and the sister nearest to you in age, Pat, had driven from Wisconsin to Colorado in Pat's Volkswagen bug. When we got to that place near the canyon's mouth where East Creek flows beside huge cottonwoods small beneath sandstone walls that rise rain-stained into a deep summer-blue sky, we separated from Lorraine and Pat as they unloaded the picnic basket and walked down to the creek. A golden eagle soared around and around above our heads, dark wings outspread, close enough for us to clearly make out its beak as its wheeled and wheeled. "A sign," we laughed, looking into each other's eyes, still strangers but already more than strangers.

Sandstone cliffs, an eagle,
day blazing,
love trembling toward beginning.

The True Birth of Poetry

She introduced me to African poetry first:
Powerful rhythms and sun-drenched landscapes.

I was the son of a small grocery store owner
that our family and one employee ran
seven days a week, sixteen hours a day.
I was on my way to dropping out of community college,
although I didn't know that yet,
my pretensions to becoming a real writer
drowning in the undisciplined angst of who I was.

She was exotic, blond, Scandinavian, an older woman
who had a child that ran around
in Colorado sunshine like a wild bird out of place.
She told me she had met Langston Hughes
and had prepared to enter the Peace Corps
until motherhood had changed her life
and sent her fleeing from Wisconsin to Colorado,
afraid of how her father would react to her child.

Then she showed me the poems of her little sister:

A moon
caught me
by
the throat
and searched
my pockets
for a soul
till love
screamed
across
the pencil lines
of trees

and the angst of who I was: Handicapped with bent back, book worm
   because I didn't dare try to keep up with a gang of kids my age,
   poet who had read Dostoevsky in the tenth grade but did not yet
   really understand poetry,

swirled with emotions so powerful I felt unhinged.
My God, this was a real, not a pretend, poet.
Her images burned with fevers that changed how you looked at snow:

You
smell like
wild snow

or moss:

you can hear
the moss
cling to the sides
of trees

I wrote her little sister, a year and a half older than I was, a letter.
I was putting this magazine, *The Rimrock Poets Magazine*, together.
Could we include her poetry?
A letter came back. I wrote another letter, a letter to me followed.
Soon we were writing about more than poetry,
about more than the lives we had lived up to then.
We didn't talk about tragedies and fears, but about present and future
    dreams, the spirit of who we thought we really were.

After all these years later, when life seems so short
as time disappears into sunsets and sunrises that come and go,
casualties that lead from one moment to another
seem mysterious, filled with coming and going
that flows into meaning that gives substance to who we are.

I was not ready to meet the love of my life when I met her.
I was too insubstantial, too involved with an unformed self
that only half believed someone so crippled physically and emotionally
could find any measure of joy in life.

But in the crucible of meeting, running away from love,
then, finally, coming to a moment in an empty field bathed with
    moonlight
when a future seemed plausible for the first time,
I began to be who I was to someday become,
and poetry ran wild in my veins.

Cryptic Moon

The moon rose over Grand Mesa's dark blue rim
dark red, a presence hanging ominously vast
above our heads, the hills around us, dim
from fading light, now eerie, light recast
into a land of shadows burned with burnished red
that made the piñon's stillness bristle gloom
and rocks elongate as they shined and bled
across a landscape rising toward the moon.

We walked, hand clasped in hand, our love intense,
into the weirding light, our senses shocked
by how the day had disconcerted sense,
transmuted time, the spirit of the rocks.

We walked in silence as the red, red moon
compressed to gold, then silver, a cryptic rune.

The Poet and the Artist

Inside the trailer sitting by a ditch,
the mixing bowl still clinging to the dough
that went into the oven hours before
to make the fresh-bread smell of early morning,
the poet, young, sat down to write a poem.
She pursed her lips and pledged a word to paper,
stopped, got up from the folding table, looked
as if a storm had started brewing thunderheads
behind her eyes, crossed out the word she'd written,
put down another word, and then another,
decided that the first line was not right,
crossed out the line, and searched for fire, for stone
grown out of ancient trees into a rainbow
of carbon, agate, life long gone remembered
in music swelled out of the lines she wrote.

She worked for hours, the crossed-out words and lines
alive, then petrified into oblivion
across a half a dozen pages, images
half formed, then tossed away into the blaze
of other images born from the dance
of words dredged out of who she was inside
where light burned, thoughts danced, deep emotions swirled.

When, at long last, the poem was done, she shrugged,
picked up a stick of charcoal, stormed a portrait
of Pasternak, romantic, breathing, flaring
into his Russian world, onto a newsprint pad

and finished faster than the morning's bread had cooled.

Pasternak

A drawing by Ethel Mortenson (Davis), 1968

A Lover's Song

We strung along a priceless string of stars
And made the moon a pendant just for show.
I cut the night into a dress, the bars
Of moonlight setting stars and dress aglow.

You laughed with love deep in your doe-brown eyes.
You swirled the universe upon your hem.
As dizzy as a lover filled with love's first lies,
I watched your eyes grow dazzled by your gems.

Then, with a shrug, your dress fell to the ground.
The night became a carpet at your feet.
Stars glistened in a heap; their skies cut down.
The moon gleamed silver-cold without your heat.

We swirled together deep into the night,
Our years illuminated, blazing light.

Epilogue

Inside a Whorling Vortex

I saw my mother and father last night.
Sky was a deep purple,
and I felt whorling vortexes around me.
My dad was sixty-eight and my mother ninety-eight.
Exuding love, they were trying to adjust their ages
so, they'd know each other again.
Time and space had slipped between who they'd once been.

Even though they'd found each other,
my mom had lived years and experiences
my dad had never known.
I sensed, trying as hard as they could,
they were struggling to shift their times
into a tapestry that made sense to either of them.

They'd made progress, my mom getting younger,
losing dimming in her eyes and deep confusion
dominating her the last time I'd seen her in the nursing
    home.
My dad had grayed his hair
and imagined how life had been without him there.
He'd aged the way he'd once thought he would.

Then time would shift.
They were not who they'd been.

Not sure they sensed me,
I reached out from wherever I was
and tried to weave the love they'd had
into a tapestry, erasing time,
and the river I had always thought time was.

Then I realized, they weren't inside a there.
I had no idea where I was in space or time.

What My Father and Mother Said

"Any good worker is worth his hire," my father told me.
"Patience is the best way to get along in the world."

He also said,
"That meal, Mama, was finer than frog's hair sitting
     on a split wood fence and blowing in the wind."
     And he always said,
"You're not the only pebble on the beach, son. Remember
     that."

My mother always said,
     "Don't mix bad seeds with the good
and don't run around all night like a dog
trying to catch the end of its tail."

She also said,
"Say please before you ask and remember your manners
     at the table,
and for bells shells, don't go reading books in bed!"

Let there be moonlight and starlight and sunlight.
Let there be stones and moss and trees.
That's what my father and mother said.

ABOUT THE AUTHOR

Thomas Davis has spent his career in Indian education as the President or Chief Academic Officer of five different tribal colleges or universities. He also was important in the founding of both the Menominee Indian School District, College of the Menominee Nation, Advanced Networking for Minority Serving Higher Education Institutions, and the World Indigenous Nations Higher Education Consortium.

He has published two books of poetry, two epic poems, seven novels, and a book of nonfiction. He has also co-edited two poetry anthologies and had poetry, essays, and short stories published in a range of magazines and literary journals. He's had two plays performed by amateur drama groups. His literary honors include the Edna Ferber Fiction Award and an Outstanding Achievement in Poetry Award for his book, *Meditations on the Ceremonies of Beginnings*, from the Wisconsin Library Association.

He and his wife, the artist and poet Ethel Mortenson Davis, are the proprietors of Four Windows Press and are also the current Poet Laureates in Door County, Wisconsin. They have two daughters, Sonja and Mary, a son, Kevin, who died from cancer when he was 27 years old, four grandchildren, Sophia and Phoebe Wood and Will and Joey Bingen, and one great grandson, Rafa.